The Woman as Survivor

American University Studies

Series I
Germanic Languages and Literature

Vol. 85

PETER LANG
New York · San Francisco · Bern
Frankfurt am Main · Paris · London

Aleidine Kramer Moeller

The Woman as Survivor

The Evolution of the Female Figure in the Works of Heinrich Böll

PETER LANG
New York · San Francisco · Bern
Frankfurt am Main · Paris · London

Library of Congress Cataloging-in-Publication Data

Moeller, Aleidine Kramer
    The woman as survivor : the evolution of the female
figure in the works of Heinrich Böll / Aleidine Kramer
Moeller.
        p. cm. — (American university studies. Series I,
Germanic languages and literature ; vol. 85)
    Includes bibliographical references.
    1. Böll, Heinrich, 1917-1985—Criticism and interpretation.
2. Women in literature. 3. Böll, Heinrich, 1917-1985—
Religion. I. Title. II. Series: American university
studies. Series I, Germanic languages and literatures ;
vol. 85.
PT2603.O394Z7249   1991   833'.914—dc20   91-17714
ISBN 0-8204-1131-0   CIP
ISSN 0721-1392

Die Deutsche Bibliothek-CIP-Einheitsaufnahme

Moeller, Aleidine Kramer:
The woman as survivor : the evolution of the female
figure in the works of Heinrich Böll / Aleidine Kramer
Moeller.—New York; Berlin; Bern; Frankfurt/M.; Paris;
Wien: Lang, 1991
    (American university studies : Ser. 1, Germanic
languages and literature ; Vol. 85)
    ISBN 0-8204-1131-0
NE: American university studies / 01

The author gratefully acknowledges
Verlag Kiepenheuer & Witsch GmbH &
Co. for permission to reprint from the
works of Heinrich Böll.

The paper in this book meets the guidelines for permanence and durability
of the Committee on Production Guidelines for Book Longevity of the
Council on Library Resources.

∞

Table of Contents

Chapter Six

Chapter One

Introduction

The absurdity of war and its aftermath stands at the core of Heinrich Böll's fiction. While his international reputation as a writer rests on the powerful depictions of Germany's war guilt and the greed and complacency created by the *Wirtschaftswunder*, central to his works is the relationship between a man and a woman. Böll has said "im Grunde interessieren mich als Autor nur zwei Themen: die Liebe und die Religion."[1] Critics have concerned themselves variously with Böll's political involvement, his religious-philosophical views and his narrative technique.[2] Hailed by some as the "Rabelais of postwar Germany,"[3] others have suggested that he be viewed as an impressionist.[4] He was internationally recognized for his literary achievement in 1972 with the awarding of the Nobel Prize. With the appearance of *Gruppenbild mit Dame*, significant interest in Böll's female characters was awakened. Yet what has been neglected in the Böll criticism thus far is a thorough investigation of the development of the role of the female figure. This study of the complex and often enigmatic nature of the female characters in the entire prose corpus to date will attempt to fill that need.

The critics dealing with Böll's women characters to this point have

---

[1] "Interview von Reich-Ranicki (1967)" in *Heinrich Böll: Aufsätze Kritiken Reden,* (Cologne: Kiepenheuer and Witsch, 1967), p. 510.

[2] Böll's narrative technique has been compared variously to that of J. D. Salinger, Franz Kafka, Dostoievsky, Thomas Mann, Charles Dickens and Ernest Hemingway by the following critics respectively: Klieneberger, Potoker, Plant, Heiney, R. Locke. See Bibliography.

[3] *The Christian Science Monitor*, October 20, 1966, p. 10.

[4] "Briefly Noted," *The New Yorker*, October 7, 1967, p. 161.

either limited their discussion to a single work[5] or have included only the early works in their analyses.[6] More recently studies have been undertaken of Böll's male "Ich-Erzähler" and its relationship to his female protagonists. Karin Huffzky analyzes the two main male characters in Böll's recent novels, Hans Schnier (*Ansichten eines Clowns*) and the *Verf.*, (*Gruppenbild mit Dame*).[7] Suzanne Hirsch has done an interesting study, seeking to demonstrate that Böll's preoccupation with the problems of war and the restoration undergoes a steady development in an increasingly positive and social response to the economic and psychological problems of postwar Germany. She finds the basis of this development in the female protagonists of Böll's four novels dealing with war and restoration, *Und sagte kein einziges Wort, Haus ohne Hüter, Billard um halbzehn, and Gruppenbild mit Dame.*[8] These works are invaluable. What has been overlooked, however, is that Böll's portrayal of women has an evolutionary character, that can only be understood by a thorough examination of the development of the female figures in all of Böll's fiction. This development from a woman who is almost "exclusively a

---

[5]These critics include: Margaretha Deschner, "Böll's Lady: A New Eve," in *University of Dayton Review*, 11 ii (1973) pp. 11-23; H. M. Waidson, "Heroine and Narrator in Heinrich Böll's Gruppenbild mit Dame," In *FMLS*, 9 (1973), pp. 123-31; Gertrud Pickar, "The Impact of Narrative Perspective on Character Portrayal in Three Novels of Heinrich Böll, Billard um halbzehn, Ansichten eines Clowns, and Gruppenbild mit Dame," in *U. of Dayton Review*, Vol. 11, 1974, pp. 25-35.

[6]David Bronsen, "Böll's Women: Patterns in Male-Female Relationships, *Monatshefte*, LVII (1965), p. 292.

[7]Karin Huffzky, "Die Hüter und ihr Schrecken von der Sache: Das Mann-Frau Bild in den Romanen von Heinrich Böll," in Hanno Beth, ed. *Heinrich Böll: Eine Einführung in das Gesamtwerk in Einzelinterpretationen* (Regensburg: Scriptor Verlag, 1975), pp. 29-54.

[8]Suzanne Hirsch, "Heinrich Böll's Female Trinity and the Restauration: Evolution of a Response," Diss. Texas-Austin, 1976.

mover behind the scenes"[9] to a person of central importance. Böll's titles alone allude to the changing role of woman in his earlier works *Und sagte kein einziges Wort, Gruppenbild mit Dame,* to his final work *Frauen vor Flußlandschaft.*

In Böll's early works, women are not without influence, but a woman in these novels and stories "exerts her influence for good or evil on the man with whom she is intimately involved, and he in turn translates the influence into action through his dealings with society."[10] Critics generally agree that woman is restricted to a role of secondary importance, that she is often sketched in "bare outline."[11]

Nowhere in these early works, up through and including *Ansichten eines Clowns,* is there to be found a career woman, or any woman for that matter, who occupies a position of authority or leadership. Up to this point Böll's standard "good" woman is non-intellectual, normally passive, someone who intervenes into her husband's affairs only when "the conflicting demands of life threaten to engulf him."[12] She has a unique and most important function in that she is able to guide her man into remaining true to his inner convictions when society threatens to force a compromise of those principles. Love forms the core of her existence and through this love she becomes the conscience of her male lover.[13]

In a certain sense these early women take on the role of the non-conformist. In helping their men remain true to their inner convictions, these women aid in the struggle to remain an individual in a mass society.

---

[9]Bronsen, p. 292.

[10]Ibid., p. 292.

[11]Wilhelm Johannes Schwarz, *Heinrich Böll, Teller of Tales,* trans. Alexander and Elizabeth Henderson (New York: Ungar Publishing Co., 1969), p. 73.

[12]Bronsen, p. 299.

[13]Ibid., p. 299.

4

Of course, Böll also creates women who are readily willing to compromise their principles if they can benefit materially, but these women are depicted in a very negative light. Hans Schnier's mother (*Ansichten eines Clowns*) serves as an example of such a negative female character.

With the appearance of Böll's following two works, *Gruppenbild mit Dame* (1971) and *Die verlorene Ehre der Katharina Blum* (1974) however, the woman ceases to be merely the catalyst, setting her man into action, but is portrayed as an intelligent, independent, and strong individual, one who is fully capable of defending herself, forcefully if necessary. Leni Pfeiffer, the female protagonist in *Gruppenbild mit Dame*, "is his most complex baffling, intriguing protagonist to date,"[14] "wohl die menschlichste Person, die Böll je gezeichnet hat,"[15] "eine neue Dimension des Menschlichen, vielleicht ein neuer Mensch." [16]

Katharina Blum, unlike Leni Pfeiffer, is a woman alone, without a "group." In a way reserved in the earlier novels for men, she actively sets out to do away with the perpetrator of evil, a journalist (appropriately named *Töt*ges) who has succeeded in shattering her reputation. This novel is in part an allegory of a society plagued by evil and injustice. The instrument Böll proposes to redeem society is a woman. The existence of this work, especially with its even more active heroine, justifies a thorough review of the role of woman in Böll's fiction. A significant contribution of this study will be an analysis of the biblical and religious parallels associated with woman which become ever more prevelant in Böll's later works. Leni Pfeiffer in *Gruppenbild mit Dame* is identified with Eve, her closest friend Margret with Mary Magdalene, Leni's teacher Sister Rahel

[14]Pickar, p . 25.

[15]Heinz Ludwig Arnold, "Heinrich Bölls Roman Gruppenbild mit Dame," in *Text und Kritik*, 33 (March, 1974), p. 59.

[16]Rudolf Hartung, "Heinrich Böll/Gruppenbild mit Dame," in *Neue Rundschau*, 82 (1971), p. 757.

is likened to the Virgin Mary, and Katharine Blum is unquestionably modeled on St. Catherine of Siena. The role accorded woman by the medieval Catholic Church prompted authors such as Abelard and Dante to come to her defense; Böll in the same vein, laments the role to which modern woman has been relegated, a *Lustspieleva* and *Lustspielmagdalena*.[17] He views his task as an artist to depict "was von der Gesellschaft zum Abfall, als abfällig erklärt wird,"[18] more nobly, and therefore attempts to restore woman to her innocent state through his art. This is no where more visible than in Böll's final two novels *Fürsorgliche Belagerung* and *Frauen vor Flußlandschaft*. Woman represents for Böll, according to Nielson "die Verwirklichung des Menschenseins in der Einheit von Leib, Seele und Geist...und die dadurch sensibel für das Leben sind."[19]

Like others before him, Böll celebrates woman's redemptive powers and healing ability. But this traditional image has been threatened by the war, the *Wirtschaftswunder* and pervasive materialism. Today's woman is forced to reevaluate herself and her traditional role in order to meet the new demands placed upon her.

Böll's ideal woman refuses, however, to compromise her individuality and traditional sense of morality in order to secure the riches of this world. She meets this new challenge, although sometimes in unexpected ways, and survives the encounter with her innocence and *Nächstenliebe* intact. She thus becomes for man a truly saintly model, one to which he may aspire, but can never fully realize.

---

[17]Heinrich Böll, *Frankfurter Vorlesungen* (Cologne: Kiepenheuer and Witsch, 1966), p. 111.

[18]Ibid., p. 82.

[19]Manfred Nielson, *Frömmigkeit bei Heinrich Böll.* (Annweiler: Thomas Plöger Verlag, 1987), p. 80.

Chapter Two

Böll's Early Fiction

Böll's depiction of woman in his early fiction is basically a very traditional one. All positive figures share traits of compassion and innocence and are deeply religious. The negative female characters are avaricious, primarily concerned with success and prestige. The very early works (*Der Zug war pünktlich, Wo warst du, Adam?*) concern themselves exclusively with war and its toll on men and women. The woman's role in this period is to console man and offer him some sign of hope in what is otherwise meaningless existence. Love relationships cannot flourish because war separates lovers, oftentimes through death. The early post-war novels portray war widows (*Haus ohne Hüter*) and wartorn families (*Und sagte kein einziges Wort*). Women are faced with the responsibility of raising their own families without the support of their husbands or the Church.

Woman in Wartime

The title of his first major work, *Der Zug war pünktlich* (1949), reveals the key to Böll's heroes, who are taken through life "as if by a train."[1] A busy, noisy railroad station serves as a perfect metaphor for the destiny of these characters, as it reflects their loneliness and sadness, and the uncertainty of their direction. The homelessness of the passengers in the waiting room manifests the atmosphere of the world at large after the war.

Some aspect of this war experience dominates all the characters of Böll's early works. Böll's depiction of wartime has no room for heroes or the glory of patriotism. He quotes Saint Exupery in an epigraph to *Wo*

---

[1]Richard Plant, "The World of Heinrich Böll," *The German Quarterly*, 33 (1960), p. 127.

warst du, Adam?: "der Krieg ist kein richtiges Abenteuer, er ist nur Abenteuer Ersatz. Der Krieg ist eine Krankheit. Wie der Typhus."[2] The war is seen from the point of view of the common man trapped in a situation he cannot alter and which therefore, must be endured. The only escape from the harsh reality is found in a personal relationship. The central theme becomes "Liebe im Krieg."[3] War is responsible for the separation of people who share love, thereby destroying this love, the only real truth in human existence. These early works are concerned with the search

> nach Liebe und nach dem Mittel oder dem Mittler, mit dessen Hilfe die nur in Augenblicken erlebbare Liebe in der feindlichen Umwelt gegen die Kräfte der Zerstörung zu schützen, ihr Dauer zu schenken ist.[4]

Böll's first work, *Der Zug war pünktlich*, has been hailed as an "artistic tour de force, but one that cannot and should not be repeated."[5] It is the story of a young soldier, Andreas, who is on board a train taking him to the Russian front. On the train he has a very strong premonition of his impending death. He meets two fellow soldiers, dubbed *der Blonde* and *der Unrasierte*. In an attempt to escape what lies ahead of them they drink and gamble. Andreas' thoughts continually recall a French girl he had encountered in France. While serving "in einem französischem Nest hinter Amiens,"[6] Andreas briefly catches the eye of this girl, with whom he falls

---

[2]Heinrich Böll, *Wo warst du, Adam?* (Frankfurt am Main: Ullstein, 1970), p. 5.

[3]Arpád Berntath, "Zur Stellung des Romans Gruppenbild mit Dame in Böll's Werk," in *Die Subversive Madonna: Ein Schlüssel zum Werk Heinrich Bölls*, ed. Renate Matthaei (Köln: Kiepenheuer und Witsch, 1975), p. 34.

[4]Bernath, p. 34.

[5]Theodore Ziolkowski, "Heinrich Böll: Conscience and Craft," *Books Abroad*, 34 (1960), pp. 213-222.

[6]Heinrich Böll, *Der Zug war pünktlich* (Frankfurt am Main: Ullstein, 1965) p. 38.

in love "auf den ersten Blick." He recalls her eyes on many occasions thereafter: "traurige Augen von einer Farbe wie dunkel geregneter Sand; unglückliche Augen, *viel Tierisches darin und alles Menschliche."* (Emphasis added, p. 38). This momentary encounter at Amiens becomes a crucial experience in his life. Shortly thereafter he is wounded and his search for her proves fruitless. Her eyes become a symbol of hope, a sign that humanity is still possible in these desolate times.

The *Blonde* and *Unrasierte* convince Andreas to spend his last night in a Polish brothel. Here Andreas meets Olina, a Polish prostitute, who is a member of the resistance movement. His attraction for her is a repetition of the attraction he had felt for the French girl, a *Doppelgestalt*, but this time Andreas and Olina will not allow war to separate them, not even death is able to do that, for they shall die together. Olina has suffered terribly at the hands of fascists in Warsaw and has thus joined the resistance movement. According to the moral dictates of the war, they should be enemies, but their very choice of each other as lovers allows them to assert their individuality, a rare opportunity indeed in a war setting. Through their love they are able to voice their protest against the moral code of the war.

Olina has the same eyes of the French girl, "die sanften traurigen Augen" (p. 107), but ones that could smile as well. Much as in his encounter with the French girl, Andreas immediately feels united with Olina and she to him: "Sie blicken sich lange an, sehr lange, und ihre Augen versinken in einander" (p. 108).

Olina at first feels only fear and cannot even comprehend what Andreas is saying, but that fear diminishes more and more as their departure from the world draws closer. She is a music student and plays Bach on the piano. During the time she plays Bach on the piano, Andreas has mystical visions which cause him to overcome his previous fears of his impending death. It becomes for him a death in imitation of Christ's martyrdom, which will secure a final unification of Olina and himself and a reconciliation with God.[7]

It is interesting to note that the "tierische," attraction Andreas felt for the French girl becomes a "Liebe ohne Begehren" (p. 143), a spiritual love with Olina. She appears to Andreas as his sister in one of these visions during Olina's playing. It is this spirituality that allows him to come to terms with himself and die a martyr's death.

Olina has been actively fighting a cause she cannot believe in (Fascism), unlike Andreas, who has wanted to flee it, but has done nothing actively. Her meaningful life of resistance to the oppressors contrasts with the soldier's acceptance of his existence. But Olina gives up her activities, realizing that "auch wir nur die Unschuldigen morden" (p. 105). They attempt to flee, but their car is fired upon and both die. Olina repeats a biblical phrase just before her death, "wohin ich dich auch führen werde, es wird das Leben sein" (p. 153), lending an almost redemptive formula to the end.

The figure of Olina is reincarnated in the figure of an Hungarian Catholic Jewess in Böll's next major work, *Wo warst du, Adam?* Having spent a year in a convent, Ilona (whose name is an anagram of her predecessor) returns to the outside world because "der Wunsch zu heiraten und Kinder zu haben war so stark in ihr, daß er nach einem Jahr nicht Überwunden war--und sie war in die Welt zurückgekehrt."[8] She is a most successful teacher and loves life, but "was sie schmerzte, war nur dieser Wunsch nach Zärtlichkeit und Kindern, es schmerzte sie, weil sie niemanden fand" (p. 110). Many men have pursued her, but she does not feel what she calls *Überraschung* of love. The German soldier, Feinhals, is

---

[7]Bernath, p. 41.

[8]Heinrich Böll, *Wo warst du Adam?* p. 110.

able to awaken this feeling of *Überraschung* in her. He is very much in love with Ilona, "wenn er ihr Gesicht sah . . . fühlte er etwas, was er noch nie beim Anblick einer Frau gefühlt hatte; er liebte sie und wollte sie besitzen" (p. 73). Ilona is terribly afraid of Feinhals and of love. When he asks her why she is so fearful, "sind wir denn wie Tiere, daß ihr solche Angst habt?" (p. 69), she retorts with "Ja . . . Wie Wölfe . . . Wölfe, die jeden Augenblick von Liebe anfangen können" (p. 69). She is afraid of love, "weil es sie nicht gibt--nur für Augenblicke" (p. 75).

Ultimately, Ilona is taken to a concentration camp under the command of a demented officer named Filskeit. She cannot feel the fear she had experienced before, but realizes that she is "nicht mehr unter Menschen;" she turns to prayer: ". . . nicht um irgend etwas zu bekommen oder von irgend etwas verschont zu werden, nicht um einen schnellen, schmerzlosen Tod oder um Leben, betete einfach . . . zu beten füllte sie mit einer kühlen Heiterkeit" (p. 109).

Filskeit commands her to sing something and she sings the Litany of the Saints. She looks him straight in the eye and suddenly she understands the meaning of the word fear. She continues to sing beautifully and smiles "trotz der Angst" (p. 112). Filskeit cannot fathom that the Jewess Ilona can possess everything he held so dear: *Schönheit, Größe, raßische Vollendung*, combined with faith.[9] He has never been able to bring himself to kill anyone, much to his own disappointment, but now he raises the gun and empties it on her. Even though Filskeit is the master of death, he cannot manipulate her faith, love, purity and joy for life.

In this novel, death does not mean that suffering has been conquered as in *Der Zug war pünktlich*, but rather that nothing more can be done on this earth. It underscores the contrast between humanism and barbarism in wartime. The union of two people, who love each other, is no longer

---

[9]Hans Joachim Bernhard, *Die Romane Heinrich Bölls* (Berlin: Rütten & Loening, 1970), p. 54.

possible in wartime.[10]   The union between Feinhals and Ilona remains potential and does not become a reality. His encounter with Ilona has offered him a hint of hope, but one that cannot put aside the horror of reality. Feinhals recognizes before his own death:

> Sie schien gewußt zu haben, daß es besser war, nicht sehr alt zu werden und ihr Leben nicht auf eine Liebe zu bauen, die für die Augenblicke wirklich war, während es eine andere, eine ewige Liebe gab (p. 153).

In these two novels Böll characterizes wartime as a world without women. "Eine Welt von Männern ohne Frauen ist unmenschlich hart, gesellschaftlich und individuell."[11]   One of Böll's soldiers is so moved by an offering of bread by a woman on the train that he is close to sobs, but he fears his comrades would not understand:

> Aber die würden nie verstehen, daß es nicht nur wegen des Brotes war, nicht nur, weil wir die deutsche Grenze nun überschritten hatten, hauptsächlich deshalb, weil ich zum erstenmal seit acht Monaten für einen Augenblick die Hand einer Frau auf meinem Arm gespürt hatte.[12]

Böll again reiterates this sentiment in *Der Zug war pünktlich*: "Es ist furchtbar, immer nur unter Männern zu sein, die Männer sind so weibisch. Es ist sehr schön, in einem Zug mit Frauen zu fahren" (p. 67).   Several of the stories in Böll's collection *Wanderer, Kommst du nach Spa?* (*Aufenthalt in X, Die gute, alte Renee*) deal with the rare understanding that can occur between a man and a woman in time of war. *Abschied*

---

[10]*Ibid.*, p. 61.

[11]Albrecht Beckel, *Mensch, Gesellschaft, Kirche bei Heinrich Böll* (Osnabrueck: Fromm Verlag, 1966), p. 50.

[12]Heinrich Böll, *Erzählungen 1950-1970* (Cologne: Kiepenheuer and Witsch, 1973). This quote is from *Als der Krieg zu Ende war*, p. 317.

(1950), for instance, has been called a "love story in black, tenderness in the midst of horror."[13]   It is a broken conversation between an injured young war veteran and a girl enroute to Sweden to join the man she loves. She is able to escape for a "Traum," but he is forced to carry on in a war-destroyed country, which has nothing left to offer him.

Kumpel mit dem langen Haar (1947) is the story of a black marketeer who meets a young girl, who, like himself, leads a very restless and unrooted existence. The young man encounters her in the waiting room of a train station and follows her onto a train. They talk and get off the train together, but neither knows where to go, "wüsste ich nur wohin." They find hope in each other:

> Als es kühl wurde gegen Morgen, kroch ich ganz nahe zu
> ihr, und sie deckte einen Teil ihres dünnen Mäntelchens
> über mich. So wärmten wir uns mit unserem Atem und
> unserem Blut. Seitdem sind wir zusammen--in dieser
> Zeit (p. 16).

Other protagonists find ultimate relief from their loneliness, fear and alienation in death. As in *Der Zug war pünktlich*, life after death in these stories is sometimes depicted as a reunion with the loved ones. In the stories *Steh auf, steh doch auf* (1950), *Wiedersehen mit Drüng* (1950), and *Wiedersehen in der Allee* (1948), the hero finds consolation in a mystical vision of a woman who waits with a smile to take him to the life hereafter.

> der Docht war versunken, kein Zipfelchen ragte mehr
> über die wachserne Oberfläche hinaus, und doch blieb es
> hell--bis unsere erstaunten Augen Dinas Gestalt sahen,
> die durch die verschloßene Tür zu uns getreten war, und
> wir wußten, daß wir nun *lächeln* durften, und nahmen
> ihre ausgestreckten Hände und folgten ihr (Emphasis

---

[13]Gerd Kalow, "Heinrich Böll," in *Christliche Dichter der Gegenwart*, ed. Hermann Friedmann and Otto Mann (Heidelberg: Rothe, 1955), p.429.

14

added, p. 90, *Wiedersehen mit Drüng*).

A woman's smile becomes for Böll a symbol of a reunion in the hereafter:

> Dieses kleine Lächeln, das ihr getauscht habt, wird nie sterben, niemals sage ich dir es wird euer Erkennungszeichen sein, wenn ihr euch in einem anderen Leben wiederseht ein lächerliches kleines Lächeln (*Wiedersehen in der Allee*, p. 98).

Woman In Postwar Germany

Böll illuminates many postwar problems as well in this collection of stories. *Die Botschaft* (1947) gives a glimpse of a war widow and her lot after the war. A friend of the deceased husband comes to give the personal belongings to the wife and finds her with another man. He realizes the extent of the destruction of the war: "Da wusste ich, daß der Krieg niemals zu Ende sein würde, solange noch irgendwo eine Wunde blutete, die er geschlagen hat" (p. 69). He cannot blame her for her action, war is the guilty party. In a scene reminiscent of Mary Magdalene washing the feet of Christ to express her humility, the woman asks him not to judge her too severely. He retorts by kissing her on the hand "es war das erste Mal in meinem Leben, daß ich einer Frau die Hand küßte" (p. 70), a sign of his own compassion and understanding.

Although written at a much later time in Böll's career, the two stories, *Als der Krieg ausbrach* (1961/62) and *Als der Krieg zu Ende war* (1961/2) should be included here because they deal with the problem of war. *Als der Krieg ausbrach* relates the forced separation of two lovers by the war. A telephone conversation between the two is interrupted by a shouting army officer demanding ammunition on the spot. She wants to take the next train to see him off, but something stops him from telling her to come: "Sie hatte so nach Ehe geklungen, und ich wußte plötzlich, dass ich keine Lust hatte, sie zu heiraten" (p. 300). In the war he yearns for female companionship, not out of a sexual need, but simply for "Gesellschaft und keine männliche." War is depicted, much as in *Wo warst du, Adam?*, as a world without women, "unmenschlich hart."[14]

In *Als der Krieg zu Ende war*, the young soldier returning home feels very alone and out of touch with his peers and society.[15] He finds it almost impossible to communicate with anyone, "mit keinem verbindet ihn irgendeine tiefere seelische Gemeinsamkeit."[16] He first calls his wife, both are overcome with emotion upon hearing each other's voices. As he goes to the train station to meet her, he still hears his wife's voice, "die noch nie nach Ehe geklungen hatte" (p. 331). According to Böll, as soon as two people intend to make a relationship formal through an external act or bond such as marriage, "ist die eigentliche Bindung gefährdet oder schon gebrochen."[17] It appears that through compassion and love, he may be able to overcome his wish "lieber ein toter Jude als ein lebender Deutscher zu sein" (p. 319).

In these stories and novels it becomes evident that the heroes are able to overcome their weakness and state of non-communication because they receive moral strength from their wives and girlfriends. Still, the role of the female character in these early works seems to be a passive one. She is portrayed as a good woman coming from the lower classes, who is

---

[14]Beckel, p. 50.

[15]Böll reveals in a postscript to the Rowohlt edition of *Draussen vor der Tür* (1947) that his own view of war is akin to Wolfgang Borchert's view: "Die Wahrheit des Dichters, Borcherts verlorene, Gemetzel waren, dass für die Toten die Blumen der Wind nicht mehr für sie weht; dass ihre Kinder Waisen, ihre Frauen Witwen sind und Eltern um ihre Söhne trauern." Wolfgang Borchert, *Draußen vor der Tür* (Hamburg: Rowohlt, 1956), p. 119.

[16]Leopold Hoffmann, *Heinrich Böll* (Luxembourg: Sankt Paulus Drückerei, 1965), p. 42.

[17]*Interpretationen zu Heinrich Böll: Kurzgeschichten I*, (Munich: Oldenbourg Verlag, 1970), p. 22.

usually a practicing Catholic.[18]   As is seen in Ilona, her nature remains one of pure inwardness, she turns to prayer--not to another person.

In the relationship between a man and a woman, the woman bears her burden and fate without hostility, but she does not act. This is nowhere better depicted than in Böll's *Und sagte kein einziges Wort*.

This novel is Böll's first attempt to depict the state of society after World War II by focusing on a single marriage, that of Fred and Käte Bogner. Fred has returned from the war with a heightened sense of futility of existence and a colossal indifference to all those things that other men are determined to take seriously.[19]   He can see "hinter der hektischen Betriebsamkeit und dem kommerziellen Ehrgeiz des deutschen Wirtschaftswunders nur die Leere und den Horror."[20]   He attempts to escape by drinking, gambling, and finally foresaking his family, but "immer noch lastet schmerzlich die Erinnerung an den Krieg auf seinem Gemüt."[21] Fred feels society must accept responsibility for the past and finds it impossible to simply start again where he left off before the war. His resistance to conform is a protest against what Böll calls "das Weitergehen des Lebens."[22]   This refusal ultimately leads to a retreat from society, a behavior typical of an existentialist, who sees himself as an outsider.

Meanwhile, Käte bears the burden of her struggle in silence, while her male counterpart and husband, Fred, tries to come to terms with

---

[18]Bronsen, p.291.

[19]W. A. Coupe, "Heinrich Böll's *Und sate kein einziges Wort*--An Analysis," *German Life and Letters*, 17 (1963-64), p. 268.

[20]Herbert M. Waidson, "Die Romane und Erzählungen Heinrich Bölls," in *Der Schriftsteller, Heinrich Böll: eine biographisch-bibliographischer Abriß*, ed. Werner Lengning (Cologne: Kiepenheuer and Witsch, 1959), p. 45.

[21]*Ibid.*, p. 45.

[22]Heinrich Böll, "Deutsche Meisterschaft," in *Text und Kritik 33* Heinrich Böll, ed. Heinz Ludwig Arnold (Munich: Richard Boorberg, March 1974) p. 1. "Es gibt da schließlich eine Dampfwalze, die heißt: Das Leben geht weiter."

himself and the new world of the *Wirtschaftswunder*. The title of the novel itself, *Und sagte kein einziges Wort*, alludes to the passive acceptance that Käte Bogner exhibits in this novel. She has lost two children in the war and now has been robbed of her once vital husband, yet she bears her husband's instability and neuroses in complete silence, exercising no control over her destiny. She makes no attempt to coerce her husband to become a "useful" member of society, nor does she reproach his behavior. Käte is a Catholic with an unquestioning faith in God, despite the adversities she has had to suffer. She is, however, not in agreement with the official Church values. She is not an active participant in Church activities. Her religion is an internal one, rather than one based on ritual and formalism. This is made clear in that Käte finds consolation in prayer, rather than in confession to her priest. She is almost repulsed by the latter, because of his fondness for the material things in life and external pomp rather than inner piety.

It is interesting to note Käte's vehement remarks about her fellow women in this novel. She speaks very negatively against her neighbor, her landlady, and the girlfriend of the baby sitter.[23] The only woman she speaks of in a positive light is *das Mädchen*, who has lost her mother, whose father is an invalid, and whose brother is retarded.[24] Both Fred's and Käte's descriptions of her are very warm and positive ones, "Ihre Anwesenheit erfüllte mich mit Wohlbefinden und Ruhe" (Fred, p. 33). Käte's reaction upon seeing her for the first time:

> Ihr *Lächeln* fiel wie ein Zauber über mich, ich *lächelte* zurück, und so blieben wir einige Sekunden stehen, ohne uns zu bewegen, und während ich wirklich nur sie sah--

---

[23]Huffzky, p. 47.

[24]This figure is reminiscent of the "Holy Fool" from the Epistle of St.Paul, who has attained such purity of spirit that he/she has achieved liberation from the evil world and from matter.

sah ich, wie aus weiter Entfernung, auch mich, sah uns
beide dort stehen *einander zulächelnd* wie Schwestern (p.
76).

Böll once more makes use of the symbol of *lächeln* to represent hope,
"jenes Lächeln, das zwei menschliche Wesen einander schenken, zwischen
denen plötzlich die Wärme schweigenden Einverständnisses entsteht."[25]
The sign of hope occurs, however, in the *diesseits*, not in the *jenseits* as in
the past two novels, *Der Zug war pünktlich* and *Wo warst du, Adam?*
Olina, Ilona, Andreas, and Feinhals had found hope only in the *Jenseits*. In
Und sagte kein einziges Wort, it is *das Mädchen* who serves as an example
to Käte and Fred of a person who has survived the war and materialistic
society of the restoration with her Christian *Nächstenliebe* intact. She
refuses to let monetary profits or personal tragedy guide her treatment of
her fellow human being. When Fred buys rolls and butter, she is generous
with her servings: "und ich sah genau, daß es mehr als ein Achtel war, was
sie neben die Brötchen legte, es war das größte der vier Viertel" (p. 33).
The two women appear as sisters to each other because they have shared
common tragedies, not unique to them alone, but shared by all women.
Das Mädchen bears her bitter burden nobly. Christian love takes on the
burden and does not seek to get rid of the other person because he is a
burden: "bear the burden of one another's failings; then you will be
fulfilling the law of Christ" (Gal. 6:2). She regards these difficulties as
trials by God as described in Romans 5:3-5:

> We are confident even over our afflictions, knowing well
> that affliction gives rise to endurance, and *endurance*
> *gives proof of our faith, and a proved faith gives ground*
> *for hope.* Nor does this hope delude us; the love of God
> has been poured out in our hearts by the Holy Spirit,

[25]Henri Plard, "Mut und Bescheidenheit. Krieg und Nachkrieg in Werk Heinrich
Bölls," in *Der Schriftsteller Heinrich Böll: eine biographisch-bibliographischer
Abriß*, ed. Werner Lengning (Cologne: Kiepenheuer and Witsch, 1959), p. 76.

whom we have received (Emphasis added).

Through her example, *das Mädchen* redeems Käte's and Fred's marriage much like Käte's patience and love redeems Fred, "the unbelieving husband is sanctified by the believing wife" (I Cor. 7:14). This chance meeting on separate occasions of Käte and then Fred with the girl could be regarded as the turning point of the novel,[26] "vom Haß zerstört, kann sie im Unsichtbaren wiedererstehen, durch die Zärtlichkeit."[27]

Henri Plard calls the women figures like Ilona, Olina, and *das Mädchen* "Engel" in the sense of the original meaning: "Bote der Hoffnung . . . die der Vernichtung wiedersteht."[28] There are a number of examples of this "Engel" figure in Böll's short stories: the young girl with the cake in *Wanderer, kommst du nach Spa*; the women seen in the visions of the soldiers in *Steh auf, steh doch auf, Wiedersehen mit Drüng*, and *Wiedersehen in der Allee*. These women all offer hope in the hereafter, but with the appearance of *das Mädchen* this ray of hope is found in this life for the first time in Böll's works. Still these women do not have an active role in the story, "sie handeln durch das, was sie sind, nicht durch das, was sie tun."[29]

Böll also introduces a contrast figure to Käte Bogner in *Und sagte kein einziges Wort*. Frau Francke, "in many ways the exact antithesis of Käte Bogner,"[30] is the Bogners landlady and is also in charge of the housing committee that evaluates housing needs for the public. She is portrayed as a "rigorously pious keeper of the laws" of the Church, one

---

[26]*Ibid.*, p. 76.

[27]*Ibid.*, p. 76.

[28]*Ibid.*, p. 74.

[29]*Ibid.*, p. 75.

[30]Coupe, p. 244.

who receives holy communion daily. From all appearances, one would assume her to be a model Christian, but there is much more beneath the veneer. Unlike the Bogners, who are living apart, the Franckes live in lawful wedlock. It is in Frau Francke's hands that the fate of the Bogners resides. As chairperson of the housing commission, she decides not to grant a request from the Bogners for a larger dwelling, arguing that Fred is a drinker and Käte is not a faithful participant in Church activities. In reality, she is incapable of self-sacrifice. If she were to grant the Bogners an extra room, she would lose her own dining room. It is precisely because of wretched conditions of this one-room dwelling that Fred has abandoned his family.

> Unsre Wohnung ist zu klein. Das ist alles. Auch die
> Wand, die uns vor unseren Nachbarn trennt, ist zu dünn.
> Für eine größere Wohnung braucht man Geld, braucht
> man das, was sie Energie nennen, aber wir haben weder
> Geld noch Energie (p. 81).

Käte has three children and is expecting a fourth. The Franckes have no children. Frau Francke dominates her husband shamelessly, and unlike Käte, who eventually brings out Fred's good nature, she crushes any outward sign of charity. She is described as "redselig lebhaft, ohne Zärtlichkeit" (p. 22), in contrast to Käte, who is reticent and patient. Frau Francke is the object of Böll's scorn in this novel, she places external piety above love and compassion and hides behind her greed and selfishness (self-love) behind her social activities on behalf of the Church. Her name Francke, the Swiss or French coin, points to this important side of her nature: her greed.[31]

The two dominant feelings that Käte experiences throughout the novel are *Schrecken* and *Angst*, which clearly delineate her as a victim.

---

[31]James Henderson Reid, "Böll's Names," in *Modern Language Review*, 69 (1974), p. 58.

Throughout the work numerous parallels are drawn between Christ and Käte. The title *Und sagte kein einziges Wort* refers to a negro spiritual that Käte often hears on Sundays, "and he said not a mumbalin' word," referring to Christ's suffering without complaint. She, like so many of Böll's female characters, is reticent about her lot and accepts her fate as it is presented to her:

> Gekreuzigt, schweigend, ihren Mann und ihre Kinder weiterhin liebend, triumphiert Käte uber die Welt wie Christ durch sein Opfer und seine unerschütterliche Liebe über Sünde.[32]

The few things in which Käte finds consolation are prayer, "das Beten ist das einzige, was helfen könnte," and the crucifix that hangs above her door in the apartment:

> Meine Blicke gehen unsere Wände entlang, nichts findet Gnade vor meinen Augen als das Kruzifix . . . (p. 23).

The crucifix is an especially appropriate object of consolation for Käte, because the cross has always represented the basic attitude that underlies Christian thought. The horizontal and vertical bars serve as a pair of opposites underscoring the duality of the cross itself. The horizontal represents the passive principle, the world of phenomena. The vertical represents the active principle, the transcendent or spiritual world. One must choose between these two roads--penitence leading to salvation and prevarication leading to damnation.[33]

A feeling of *Schreck* overtakes her whenever she encounters hypocrisy or sanctimony:

---

[32]Plard, p. 68.

[33]J. E. Cirlot, *A Dictionary of Symbols* (New York: Philosophical Library, Inc., 1962), pp. 70-71.

> Schrecken ergreift mich, wenn ich manchmal unten im
> Keller bin, um Kohlen oder Kartoffeln zu holen, und ich
> höre sie nebenan die Gläser zählen: mit sanfter Stimme
> murmelnd, singend die Zahlen wie die Kandenzen einer
> geheimen Liturgie, und ihre Stimme erinnert mich an die
> Stimme einer betenden Nonne--und ich lasse oft meine
> Eimer im Stich, fliehe nach oben und drücke meine Kinder
> an mich, weil ich spüre, daß ich sie vor etwas behüten
> muß (p. 22).

It frightens Käte to be the object of such hatred by Frau Francke:

> Die Tatsache, Gegenstand eines solchen Haßes zu sein,
> flüßt mir Furcht ein, und ich habe Angst, den Leib Christi
> zu essen, dessen Genuß Frau Francke täglich
> erschreckender zu machen scheint. Denn der Glanz ihrer
> Augen wird immer härter. Und ich habe Angst, die
> heilige Messe zu hören . . . ich habe Angst den Pfarrer am
> Altar zu sehen (pp. 19-20).

She retreats now and again into the Church, but one "in denen kein Gottesdienst mehr stattfindet und ich empfinde den unendlichen Frieden, der von der Gegenwart Gottes ausströmt" (p. 20). To sublimate this fear and her hopeless situation, Käte retreats in the opposite manner of her husband Fred, she wages an active war against the dirt and dust in her apartment: "Dann beginne ich meinen Kampf, den Kampf gegen den Schmutz" (p. 37). Böll, in his depiction of man and woman, portrays the woman as the domestically potent, energetic one; she does the wash and cares for the children, as the man whiles away the time in non-constructive activity. The man is depicted as *nichtstuend* and *stupide*.

> Ich sehe dort hinten Frauen--gelbe Frauen an träge
> dahinfließenden Strömen Wäsche waschen . . . sehe
> schwarze Frauen in spröder Erde graben, höre das
> sinnlose und so reizvolle Getömmel *nichtstuender*
> Männer im Hintergrund, braune Frauen sehe ich, wie sie

in steinernen Trögen Körner zerstampfen, den Säugling auf dem Rücken, während die *Männer stupide* um ein Feuer hocken, die Pfeife im Munde--und meine weißen Schwestern in den Mietskasernen von London, New York und Berlin, in den dunklen Schluchten der Pariser Gassen--bittere Gesichter, die erschreckt auf die Rufe eines Trunkenboldes horchen (p. 40).

This depiction of woman and man is extended to a universal truth of humanity.

At the very core of Käte's nature is love, through this love she is able to weather her long personal crisis. She feels love for her children, her husband, and her God. "Ich sehe Freds Gesicht unerbittlich alt werdend, leergefressen von einem Leben, das nutzlos wäre und gewesen wäre, ohne die Liebe, die es mir einflößt" (p. 54). Fred says the same thing when he admits, "das einzige, was für mich spricht, ist, daß ich dich liebe" (p. 141).

Her religion, one of personal communion with God, unburdened by formalistic ritual, seems to offer something of a solution in coping with the post-war life. It is Käte then, the woman, who is afforded the role of the preservation of virtue in a society apparently at odds with virtue. Hers is the additional task of helping her man to preserve his individuality in a conforming world. Woman, who had been relegated to the role of *Kinder*, *Kirche* and *Küche*, especially under the Nazi ideology, finds herself struggling to survive, forced to seek new goals, or perish. Käte turns to the Church for consolation only to find that it is too involved in materialism and restoration to find time for individual needs. She turns inward for consolation and finds it through prayer, as Ilona before her. She provides her husband and children with spiritual and physical nourishment, which she does "without a mumbalin' word." The woman must take over as both mother and father, as is seen in Böll's next major novel *Haus ohne Hüter*.

The main characters in *Haus ohne Hüter* are two war widows and their two sons. The dilemma of their situation and their individual responses are recorded in this work. More sympathy is awarded to the two adolescent boys on the part of the reader, for they have had to suffer the most from the condemnations of their mothers' actions by both their peers and the rest of society.[34] The two female characters are Nella Bach and Wilma Brielach, each of whom has lost her husband during the war and has an eleven-year-old son. Wilma Brielach is quite poor and is dependent on her son and a series of lovers for money and companionship, respectively. She takes on lovers in hope of finding a father for her son to try to ensure a return to a normal family life. "She bears the heaviest blows of fate and the worst humiliations for the sake of her children."[35] She plans for the future and is willing to go so far as to become a baker's mistress in hopes of securing money from him to pay for some dental work she desperately needs. She actually finds him repulsive, but envisions the material gains she will secure through this union.

Nella, on the other hand, has plenty of money and need not compromise herself to survive. She refuses to accept her husband's (Rai) death at the hands of the Nazis. Like many of Böll's heroes, she has little desire to participate in life. She dwells in the past, constantly envisioning what could have been: "Jahrelang hatte sie damit verbracht, sich auszudenken, wie alles hätte kommen können."[36] She rejects remarriage or a liaison of any kind, saying that she will not be made a war widow twice and will not contribute to the senseless process

> neue Witwen aufziehen, neue Männer die abgeknallt werden, und Frauen machen können . . . damit die Witwenfabrik weiterläuft (p. 13).

---

[34] Huffzky, p. 48.

[35] Schwarz, p. 68.

[36] Heinrich Böll, *Haus ohne Hüter* (Frankfurt am Main: Ullstein Verlag, 1969).

Like Fred Bogner in *Und sagte kein einziges Wort*, she detests those who wish her to forget the past: Oh, ich haß euch alle, weil ihr zulaßt, daß *das Leben weitergeht*. Vergessen streuen über den Mord, wie man Asche über Glateis streut" (Emphasis added, p. 113). The idea of "ein neues Leben" with a new partner fills her with disdain. She alienates her own son Martin by living in this past "Traumwelt." Martin laments that his mother spends her time and energy entertaining a literary circle of friends and finds no time for him: "Andere Jungen haben Mütter, die kochten, nähten, Butterbrote schmierten, auch die unmoralischen -- aber seine Mütter kochte nur selten, nähte nie und schmierte keine Butterbrote" (p. 117). Nella's husband Rai, a poet, was killed during the war by Gäseler, a German Nazi officer. In an attempt to learn the identification of her husband's murderer, Nella has been taking part in poetry readings in the evenings. Her husband's murderer had taken a great interest in Rai's poetry, and considered himself an expert in the area. Böll thus states his view that the period of the restoration is simply an extension of the Nazi period, in that the same people are still in command and wield the power. Nella Bach and Wilma Brielach are motivated by two opposing feelings in their actions. Nella Bach is driven by hatred and revenge, whereas Frau Brielach seeks happiness and security for herself and her son through love.

Frau Brielach, however, is scorned by her neighbors because of her lack of discrimination in choosing her lovers, while Nella Bach is respected in the community. Much like Käte Bogner, Nella withdraws from society, but cannot find the peace and consolation in religion and prayer that Käte could, perhaps because Nella's driving force is a bitter hate, rather than love.

Frau Brielach is depicted by Böll as a Mary Magdalene figure, the fallen woman who eventually will be rescued through her pure heart. Like Mary Magdalene, Frau Brielach errs in a very human fashion in seeking to resume a family life and looking for companionship for the benefit of her son. She is depicted by Böll as a pure soul, one who needs others and is willing to give and receive love.

Nella Bach and Wilma Brielach share not only a common tragic past, but also a contemporary acquaintance named Albert Muchow. He was Nella's husband's best friend and has been wooing Nella over the years in an attempt to marry her and draw her out of the past and into the present. Albert is a most interesting character. He seems to be the mean between Nella Bach and Wilma Brielach, the former dwelling in the past, the latter in the future. He is seen as a very positive figure. It is interesting to note Böll's choice of Muchow as Albert's last name. Hans Heinrich Muchow is a prominent psychologist, whose area of specialization is in the area of adolescence.[37] This emphasizes perhaps Albert Muchow's role of caring for others--self-less love in looking out for the two adolescent sons of Nella and Frau Brielach. Reid sees in his name another characteristic (from *aufmucksen*, to rebel or complain), as he rebels against the status quo and attempts actively to change the situation as it exists.[38] He tells Martin, Nella's son, never to live in the past, but rather to learn from it. Rather than advocating a complete withdrawal from society, he promulgates a sincere effort to carry on the family life as best as possible. This is in contrast to both Fred Bogner's philosophy as well as Nella Bach's. In the character of Alfred Muchow, Böll allows the male to take over a role he had delegated exclusively to women in prior novels. It is Muchow who influences Frau Brielach to abandon her life with the baker and revitalizes her energy and love for her family and herself. Like Käte Bogner, he does not condemn her instability and actions, but is patient, loving and compassionate. His life does not revolve around himself, but

---

[37]Muchow at time of publication of *Haus ohne Hüter* had published *Der Lebensraum des Großtadtkindes* (1935), *Flegeljahre* (1950), and *Jugend im Wandel* (1953).

[38]Reid, p. 581.

27

around others.

The resolution to the problems of these war widows is strongly hinted at near the end of the novel. Frau Brielach, who sees her situation with the baker as hopeless, meets Albert on the stairs as she is preparing to move her things. He says he will take Heinrich and his sister to Bietenbahn, a kind of utopian retreat, despite what her plans may be. The mood of both mother and son changes from despair to hope. "Glanz der Hoffnung war im Blick der Mutter" (p. 302).

As Wilma Brielach recalls her past lovers and the men she has known, she realizes how differently she feels towards Albert: "(er) hatte sie angesehen, wie man nicht jede Frau ansieht" (p. 305). The feeling is not motivated by money or the need for companionship, but love and understanding. She communicates her feelings through a glance: "(sie) blickte Albert ins Gesicht und sah sofort, daß Albert BEGRIFF" (pp. 300-301). This *"überraschende Erkenntnis,"* which is labeled *Verheißung* in the eyes of Frau Brielach and Albert Muchow, is comparable to the concept of "das Herz berühren" in *Und sagte kein einziges Wort* as well as the *Überraschung* Ilona feels when Feinhals is near (*Wo warst du, Adam?*). In *Haus ohne Hüter* this responsibility is extended to ones fellow man and woman, as seen by Albert's feeling of responsibility for Wilma and her two children.

Gäseler ?

When she finally meets the murderer of her husband (Graseler), Nella Bach loses her feelings of hatred and revenge. The murderer cannot even recall the fact that he committed this act, he has chosen to put all matters of war, no matter how vile, out of his mind forever. Nella returns to Albert, feeling ready to make an effort to begin a new life. She is able to pull herself out of her dream, but still bears the bitterness of the wasted years she had to endure. She returns home, hoping to marry Albert. It is, however, too late for Albert and Nella, for he has chosen Frau Brielach. In this choice, Böll clearly supports an active search for a new life, built on the past and future. Albert becomes then Böll's most positive male figure; one who actively seeks to help his fellow man.

It is interesting to note the parallels between the negative characters of Frau Francke and Nella Bach. Frau Francke hides behind the façade of the Church to carry out her selfish, greedy acts. Her prime concern is herself and not others, yet in contrast to Käte, she is respected by the community because she actively participates in the formal rituals of the Church. Nella Bach retreats into the past, and is driven by revenge to seek out the murderer of her husband. Both women are led in their actions by feelings of hatred and selfishness, rather than compassion and love. It appears that Böll's ideal woman is one who can uphold virtues of love, understanding and patience. The women seem to be very traditional in their nature, and they adhere strictly to the importance of the *Kinder, Kirche* and *Küche*. Both Käte and Frau Brielach sacrifice much for their children, place family life at the center of their lives and refuse to give up hope. This is not the case with Frau Franke, who has no children, nor with Nella, who has been so caught up in her own world, that her child has had to turn elsewhere for parental affection.

Several of Böll's short stories deal with this same inability on the part of characters to proceed with life as before the war and depict their inability to relate to the age of wealth and materialism. *Die Postkarte* (1952),[39] tells of a young man who has survived the war, returns home, marries his girl and, as the novel opens, has been married to her for ten years. He returned to the job he had held prior to the war and since then has been very successful in his career. His wife had managed to keep the job open for him during the war, and had encouraged his working for the promotions he attained. As he looks at her, he wonders if he should have called her before he had left the front:

---

[39]All stories referred to in the following discussion are contained in *Heinrich Böll, Erzählungen 1950-1970* (Cologne: Kiepenheuer and Witsch, 1973).

> *immerhin* hat sie meine Stelle bei der Firma
> offengehalten, hat meinen erlöschenen Ehrgeiz, als ich
> nach Hause kam, wieder zum Leben erweckt, und *im
> G r u n d e* verdanke ich ihr, dass die
> Aufstiegsmöglichkeiten, die meine Stelle damals bot, sich
> jetzt als real erwiesen haben (p. 68, emphasis added).

His gratitude is expressed with much hesitation, as is evident in his choice of words. Since the war, he has not felt the same ambition, nor felt the pure love he felt before the war. He can no longer appreciate the joys of nature:

> Die Sonne, das Wasser und die Lustigkeit der Leute
> kommen mir falsch vor, und ich ziehe es vor, bei
> Regenwetter allein durch die Stadt zu schlendern und in
> ein Kino zu gehen, wo ich niemanden mehr küssen muß
> (p. 69).

He views his job as a *Pflicht* and nothing more, "Ich hänge nicht an ihr (Firma) und denke nicht daran, etwas für sie zu tun" (p. 69). The job, the promotions, the ambition, were all imposed upon him, not achieved through any inner conviction on his own. He resents his wife for her interference. When women become involved in the business world or interfere with a man's world, they are depicted in a negative light by Böll. Their interference and advice is only welcomed in the domestic realm, not the business realm.

    Die blaße Anna (1953) is another view of a young soldier returning from the war, but unlike in *Postkarte*, here the young man is totally broken in spirit. He has lost his parents in the war. They have left him enough money to live on. He does not feel a sense of *Pflicht* to make a living and "lag . . . auf dem Bett, rauchte und wartete und wußte nicht, worauf ich wartete. Arbeiten zu gehen, hatte ich keine Lust" (p. 95). His thoughts drift back to a young pretty girl he had often seen prior to the war. When he learns of her facial disfigurement, the result of an air raid, he reaches out for her. As he opens the door, "wußte ich, daß ich Anna gewonnen hatte . . . legte meine Hand auf Annas Schulter und versuchte zu *lächeln*" (p. 99). The smile is once again symbolic of the ray of hope that is offered through a loving human relationship. As in *Und sagte kein einziges Wort*, this hope is offered in the *Diesseits*.

When women dominate their men and become involved in the business world, they take on masculine qualities and lose their womanhood (innocence, compassion, love and understanding). Such is the case with Bertha in *Wie in schlechten Romanen*. She has invited a prospective contractor and his wife over for dinner to get the two men to make an arrangement to secure an engineering contract for her husband. When nothing comes of it, she secures the contract through a bribe. In reality he had already secured the job because his bid was the lowest. The two women agree on a mutual bribe and the contract is secured. Bertha's husband quickly learns her business methods and morals. But like the husband in *Die Postkarte*, he does not feel the same way toward his wife. He feels almost an aversion to her:

> Ich blickte auf Berthas kleine bräunliche Hände, mit denen sie sicher und ruhig steuerte. Hände, dachte ich, die Schecks unterschreiben und auf Mayonnaisetuben drücken, und ich blicke höher--auf ihren Mund und spürte auch jetzt keine Lust, ihn zu *küssen* (Emphasis added, p. 187).

The *Küssen*, usually an act of affection, becomes an act of deceit, alluding perhaps to the Judas kiss. The same symbol was used in *Die Postkarte*, "wo ich niemanden mehr küssen muss." Both of these men have arrived at their material and professional success through their wife's ambition. They begin to feel alienated from their wives and society. When women

31

are guided by desires of wealth, prestige and position, without regard for
a moral code, or the husband's own convictions, they are depicted in a very
negative light. The philosophy of these women is summed up by Bertha:
"Das Leben besteht daraus, Kompromisse zu schließen und Konzeßionen
zu machen" (p. 186). Böll cannot tolerate a compromise of any kind when
principles are at stake.

The moral antithesis to Bertha is Franziska in *Zum Tee bei Dr.Borsig*
(1955) a radio play written a year before *Wie in schlechten Romanen*.
Franziska prevents Robert, a talented young poet, from exploiting his
artistic talent commercially. The action of the play concerns the attempts
of a large pharmaceutical firm, headed by Dr.Borsig, to hire Robert as an
advertising consultant. With his fresh and creative ideas they hope to
increase their profits on a product for which there is no consumer need.
They hope to create a market for this product, with which they have
overstocked in their warehouse. Robert is invited over for tea to discuss
his future with the company. Franziska, Robert's fianceé, is strongly
against his giving up his literary talents in order to attain financial
security. She represents the counter position of Borsig, in rejecting the
materialist ethos. Her feelings emanate from an interior purity and
sensitivity. Robert's conflict arises between the financial security and the
morality of a career in which he is advocating the sale of a worthless
product. Franziska is instrumental in his decision to reject the offer and
refuse to compromise his artistic integrity. Franziska is the one who is
totally incapable of compromising her ideals and helps Robert to remain
true to his ideals in time of wavering:

> Roberts Entschluß wird . . . durch das Vertrauen seiner
> Geliebten, die ihn seiner wahren Berufung behalten will,
> die ihn sich selbst, dem erdnahen Erlen der
> unverfälschten Existenz bewahren mochte.[40]

---

[40]Hoffmann, p. 59.

Bertha is the exact contrast to Franziska. Bertha's primary concern lies not with her husband's convictions or principles, but the monetary gains she will secure. As a result, Bertha and her husband become estranged from each other, yet Franziska and Robert live happily after.

One could conclude then, that man and woman can survive both the scars of war and the equally oppressive materialistic society, if one is able to remain true to one's principles and ideals. This, according to Böll, is not possible without a loving relationship, usually with a fellow human being. This love can, however, also find expression in the love of God, as is evidence in Böll's stories *Kerzen für Maria* (1950) and *Das Abenteuer* (1950). In Kerzen für Maria a man is doing all he can "um mir eine Existenz zu gründen, wie die Leute so schön sagen: etwas zu tun, das Geld einbringt" (p. 154). He attempts to sell candles, but is unsuccessful. He enters a church and attempts to pray, but is unable to do so: "ich fühlte mich hart, nutzlos, schmutzig, reuelos, nicht einmal eine Sünde hatte ich vorzuweisen" (p. 160). He views a statue of the Virgin Mary, "das Gesicht der Mutter Gottes war grob, aber *lächelnd*," and he immediately regrets not having a heavier load of candles in his suitcase. He lights all his candles "bis der ganze Tisch mit unruhig flackernden Lichtern bedeckt war" (p. 160). He makes his way to the train station, "und nun erst . . . fielen mir alle meine Sünden ein, und mein Herz war leichter als je" (p. 160). Böll once again lifts the burden from his hero's heart through the most compassionate among women, the Virgin Mary, who bears a smile.

The plot of *Das Abenteuer* is much the same. A young man goes to confession to bare his soul of the guilt he feels for having committed adultery. He can find no relief from his guilt through the priest or prayer: "Er versucht zu beten, aber die Worte fielen in ihn zurück wie stumpfes Geröll" (p. 14). As he leaves the church, he sees

daß in der dunklen Ecke neben dem Seiteneingang nun
Kerzen brannten vor dem Muttergottesaltar . . . ihr
Schein schaukelte die Silhouette einer alten, kleinen Frau
an die Wand des Mittelschiffs . . . ein flüchtiges Denkmal,
das die stumpfen Gipsfiguren überdeckte und über den
Rand des Daches hinauszuwachsen schien" (p. 14).

Through this contact with compassionate womanhood, even in symbolic
form, his feelings of guilt and hopelessness are lifted from him. Böll's
choice of the Virgin Mary as the representative of the spiritual realm is
most appropriate. The Virgin has remained a picture of tenderness,
womanhood, motherhood and compassion. To the men in the
aforementioned stories, she becomes a ray of light in their dark existence,
symbolized by the candles. A candle has a mystical quality about it, it
shatters the surrounding darkness and helps one to find truth, spiritual
truth. Hence, if it were not for the spiritual (candle), life (darkness) would
have no truth or meaning. Modern man, after the desolation of war, can
better identify with a loving and tender mother than with a sentencing
abstract male God.

With the appearance of Böll's collection of short stories *Nicht nur zu
Weihnachtszeit* (1952), Böll's subject matter changes significantly and shifts
from an emphasis on outrage and lamentation to one of satire. The
problem of man's isolation and alienation are still present, but post-war
society, rather than the war, becomes the culprit. His stories expose the
greed and injustice of a society whose success is measured by position,
prestige and wealth. Through the use of satire the author is able to gain
more of a distanced stance:

Aber wir wollen es so sehen wie es ist mit einem
menschlichen Auge, das normaleweise nicht ganz trocken
und nicht ganz ist, sondern feucht--und wir wollen daran
erinnern, daß das lateinische Wort für Feuchtigkeit

Humor ist--, ohne zu vergessen, daß unsere Augen auch trocken werden können oder naß; daß es Dinge gibt, bei denen kein Anlaß für Humor besteht.[41]

Through these satires, which are ranked among Böll's most successful works,[42] he is able to attack the elements of society that he detests most through humor. The absurdities are emphasized by Böll's unusual choice of professions for his eccentric heroes. The narrator of *Der Mann mit den Messern* (1848) is the assistant to a knife thrower, he is the man at whom the knives are thrown. *An der Brücke* (1949) revolves around a man who counts the number of people who cross the bridge. *Der Lacher* (1952) is about a man who laughs for a living for a radio station, thereby sparking laughter in the audience. *Bekenntnis eines Hundefängers* (1953) is about a man who looks for unregistered dogs. *Es wird etwas geschehen* (1954) is narrated by a man who leaves his present job to beome a professional mourner. *Der Wegwerfer* (1957) concerns a man whose job is to discard junk mail for people. These jobs reflect the feeling of shallowness that the materialistically oriented society holds for Böll, a world where even mourning and laughter are no longer spontaneous. Each individual above does manage, however, to preserve a small bit of his individuality by indulging in an act of private rebellion. The man at the bridge refuses to count a girl who regularly crosses the bridge. The dog catcher overlooks a few unregistered dogs and his own dog is not registered. Their private and individual revolt leaves room for a bit of individuality and independence.

Böll's positive female figures all act out of spontaneity, "alles was man für richtig findet, soll man sofort tun."[43] If man or woman acts in

---

[41]Heinrich Böll, *Hierzulande: Aufsätze zur Zeit* (Munich: Deutscher Taschenbuch Verlag, 1963), p. 133.

[42]James Henderson Reid, *Heinrich Böll: Withdrawal and Re-Emergence* (London: Oswald Wolff, 1973), p. 62.

[43]Heinrich Böll, *Nicht nur zur Weihnachtszeit* (Munich: Deutscher Taschenbuch Verlag, 1966), p. 163.

accordance with this mandate, they find happiness and satisfaction.

Hedwig Muller, the female protagonist of *Das Brot der frühen Jahre*, acts in accordance with this ethical dictate. This novel has been described as Böll's "erste umfangreichste Liebesgeschichte."[44] Walter Fendrich, a twenty-three year old appliance repairman, encounters a young woman, Hedwig Muller, who arrives in town in order to study at the Teachers' Training College. This encounter triggers a rebirth for Walter Fendrich, and he commences a "new life." A parallel to the redemptive power given to woman by Dante comes to mind. Like Beatrice, Hedwig brings a new life to Fendrich. In Böll's *Gruppenbild mit Dame*, this redemption is extended to a group, all of whom win a "new life" upon contact with Leni Pfeiffer.

Böll once more employs the railroad as a metaphor of life in his description:

> Später dachte ich oft darüber nach, wie alles gekommen wäre, wenn ich Hedwig nicht am Bahnhof abgeholt hätte: ich wäre in ein anderes Leben eingestiegen, wie man aus Versehen in einen anderen Zug steigt, ein Leben, das mir damals, bevor ich Hedwig kannte, als ganz passabel erschien.[45]

As a youth, Walter had been poor and was forced to steal bread in order to survive. His life since that time has centered upon work for the sake of money, and what it can buy. He has become involved with his boss's daughter Ulla Wickweber, who represents security to Walter. All he has to do is to follow the ambitious plans she has conceived for him and he will succeed. Ulla sees Fendrich as a competent repairman, who as her husband will take over her father's business. Walter is sent to meet

---

[44]Waidson, "Die Romane und Erzählungen Heinrich Bölls," p. 48.

[45]Heinrich Böll, *Das Brot der frühen Jahre* (Frankfurt am Main: Ullstein, 1963), p. 6.

Hedwig at the train station and at first sight she has a profound effect on him:

> Dieses Gesicht ging tief in mich hinein, drang durch mich hindurch wie ein Prägstock, der statt auf Silberbarren auf Wachs stößt, und es war, als würde ich durchbohrt, ohne zu bluten (p. 45).

She feels his desire for her and yields without hesitation, although this is not in keeping with her normal temperament, for she is anything but flighty. She intuitively feels and understands his needs and stays at his side.

Walter Fendrich is most dissatisfied with his work and life until he meets Hedwig. This "instantaneous and reciprocal love enables him to transform a diffuse dissatisfaction with prevailing values into a positive philosophy of life."[46] Falling in love has a purifying effect on Walter, it enables him to rise to a new moral valuation of himself and others.[47]

Basically then, we have a man caught between two women. Ulla is depicted as a levelheaded, pragmatic woman, with an acute appreciation for money. She sees Walter as an acceptable successor to her father, her main criterion for a husband. Fendrich has, until his meeting with Hedwig, passively submitted to her and her values. The Wickwebers, like the Franckes in *Und sagte kein einziges Wort*,[48] are successful people who attend church on a regular basis and command respect from society. Ulla's father is typical of the type of person produced by Germany's *Wirtschaftswunder*; he does not see the exploitation of his workers as a

---

[46]Robert A. Burns, *The Theme of Non-Conformism in the Works of Heinrich Böll* (Warwick: University of Warwick Occasional Papers in German Studies, 1973), p. 28.

[47]Waidson, *Die Romane und Erzählungen Heinrich Bölls*, p. 48.

[48]Burns, p. 29.

contradiction to his piety. This exploitation is acceptable to society when a material profit is realized.

> Böll shows that the real basis of social justice has been obscured, in that a person whose main priority is the maximization of profit is viewed as a just and honest member of both the Church and society.[49]

The world of Hedwig Muller is quite different. Although she is described in fragmentary terms by Böll, her nature radiates something that need not be written for the reader to understand. She introduces Walter to deeper values than the material security achieved by working at a job he detests. Both Hedwig and Walter become non-conformists in rejecting the institution of religion and marriage. The virtues of one's fellow man and humanity have lost their meaning in institutionalized religion, as seen by the Wickwebers. Hedwig and Walter find within themselves all the spirituality they need.

Upon discovering Hedwig and Walter together in Walter's room, his landlady asks them to leave. Walter attempts to explain his position:

> "Es gibt Nothochzeiten," sagte ich "wie es Nottaufen gibt." "Ja," sagte sie "das sind so Tricks. Wir sind nicht in der Wüste und sind nicht in der Wildernis, wo es keine Priester gibt," "Wir," sagte ich, "wir beide sind in der Wüste, und wir sind in der Wildernis, und ich sehe weit und breit keinen Priester, der uns trauen würde" (p. 148).

The formalistic rituals appear meaningless to them. Like Fred and Käte, they seem to be on the outside looking in. Just as Fred shows his disapproval of society and its values by leaving his family and wandering from job to job, Hedwig and Walter do not want to lend their approval to so corrupt a society by "legitimizing" their marriage in a church. Hedwig

---

[49]*Ibid.*, p. 30.

is able to awaken in Walter a new spirituality and deeper real values much as Käte is able to preserve Fred's spirituality and reunite the family. These women, through their genuine love and compassion for their men, introduce and maintain very deep and lasting values in their lives and initiate a rebirth in the lives of others.

Katharina Mirzow (*Im Tal der donnernden Hufe*, 1956) displays the same type of generous and instinctive womanhood as Hedwig and Franziska. She acts spontaneously to that which seems right to her, even if it is against the moral code of society. "Sie war das Mädchen, das getan hatte, was man nicht tut" (p. 239).

Katharina and Paul are both adolescents who are becoming aware of their own sexuality. Paul is torn between the world of childhood and approaching manhood. He feels alienated, he has been brought up to think that his awakening sexual desire is sinful. He is overcome with guilt and contemplates suicide. His conflict is symbolically revealed by the white and red tiles on the floor of the church. The white represents the purity and the red is symbolic of passion. Through Katharina he realizes that sexual love is good and she has a healing effect on him. In this encounter with Katharina, he breaks through society's barriers to find his own morality.

> Sie überzeugt ihn durch ihre eigene Schönheit und durch
> ihre Auffaßung, daß man dem Überirdischen besser durch
> das Leben als durch den Tod dienen könne, von der
> Sinnlosigkeit des Selbstmordes.[50]

He turns his pistol away from himself and directs it toward a neon beer advertisement, representative of the cold, impersonal society, the real culprit.

Sexual love is viewed as a spiritual act as well as a physical one:

---

[50]Hoffmann, p. 32.

Es ist mir unmöglich, das, was man irrigerweise die körperliche Liebe nennt, zu verachten, sie ist die Substanz eines Sakraments.[51]

As Katharina is on board the train heading for Vienna, Paul fires a few shots as a final farewell. Through her help and his friend Griff, Paul has become strong enough to voice his own protest against a cold and imposing society. Paul prefigures the active female that appears in Böll's latest work, *Die verlorene Ehre der Katharina Blum*. Whereas Paul aims his gun merely at a representative of the unjust society, Katharina Blum destroys the actual source of it. The intermediary stage of this active female is seen in Böll's next major novel *Billard um halbzehn* in the figure of Johanne Fähmel.

Restorative Society and Its Aftermath

Billard um halbzehn traces three generations of a German family, the Fähmels: "a family of dissenters who judge contemporary Germany against the ideal of a just Christian society that remains uppermost in their consciousness."[52]   Even the name "Fähmel," from the Latin word *familia*,[53] emphasizes the importance that family bonds will play in the novel.

The action is again restricted to a single day, beginning at 9:30 a.m. and closing in the early evening hours, much as in the last novel, *Das Brot der frühen Jahre*. It takes place on September 8, 1958, on the occasion of Heinrich Fähmel's eightieth birthday. By means of recollection and thoughts on the part of a variety of narrators in the novel itself, the reader catches a glimpse of five decades of German history; the days of the Kaiser, the Weimar Republic, the Nazi regime and the Adenauer era. In

---

[51]Henirich Böll, *Hierzulande*, p. 29.

[52]Theodore Ziolkowski, "Albert Camus and Heinrich Böll," in *Modern Language Notes*, 77 (1962), p. 294.

[53]Reid, "Böll's Names," p. 581.

prior novels Böll preferred either a dual narrative perspective (Käte and Fred Bogner), or quintuple perspective (Martin, Heinrich, Nella Bach, Wilma Brielach, Alfred Muchow). In this novel, Böll has employed a number of narrators, who depict or describe in detail the Fähmel family, specifically Robert Fähmel. The reader sees Robert from a myriad of perspectives: Leonore (Robert's secretary), Johanna and Heinrich (parents), Schrella (brother-in-law), Hugo and Marianne. It is interesting to note that the image of Robert presented is always the same. This "characterization by repetition" is also true of the other characters in the novel, but not to such an extent.[54]

Böll has also shifted for the first time to a bourgeois environment, a family of architects. Heinrich was commissioned to erect St. Anthony's Abbey, a commission which secures prestige and fame for his family. He marries Johanna Kilb soon after completion of this commission and encounters several tragedies. He loses a son and daughter at a very early age, but two of his sons survive childhood. Otto is a fervent Nazi, quite an enigma in the Fähmel household, as the others are all opposed to Nazism. Otto is killed in battle, leaving his brother Robert as sole survivor. Robert marries Edith and they have two children, Joseph and Ruth. Joseph is presently engaged to marry Marianne, whose parents were strict Nazi adherents. Other characters of significance are Schrella, Edith's brother, who joined the resistance movement and was forced to flee to England to escape execution. He returns twenty-two years later. Nettlinger, the man responsible for Schrella's capture, is a Nazi adherent and now a man of some influence both in politics and the Church. Hugo is the bellboy in the hotel where Robert Fähmel plays billiards every day at 9:30.

In this novel Böll is concerned with the problem he alluded to in *Haus ohne Hüter* in the figure of Alfred Muchow. Alfred takes Martin to the place where he and his companion were tortured and his friend (Martin's

---

[54]Pickar, p. 27.

father) was murdered. He warns Martin never to forget the past, but rather to learn from it. This appears to be Böll's main concern in *Billard um halbzehn,* a "jeremiad directed against the resurgence of conscienceless nationalism in Germany of 1958."[55] Karl Migner goes so far as to say "es kommt darauf an, zu zeigen, daß sich die Rollen im Übergang von der Hitler-Diktatur zur bundesrepublikanischen Demokratie keineswegs geändert haben,"[56] a thesis Böll illustrates even more vividly in *Gruppenbild mit Dame.*

Central to the novel is the dichotomy between two groups Böll dubs "Büffel" and "Lämmer." The lambs are figures of innocence, whose ideals are in opposition to contemporary society, they are nonconformists in their refusal to comply with the material world and are cognizant of its shallow pretensions. They are selfless in their love for their fellow man and become the victims of a predatory society. They are not necessarily as meek as the name lamb may seem to imply, as seen later in the characters of Johanne Fähmel and Katharina Blum. Böll makes use of the *leitmotiv* phrase *"Mitleidend bleibt das ewige Herz doch fest"*[57] (Emphasis added). Böll stresses that compassion must be allied with strength of mind.[58]

The buffalo are the opportunists, materialists, whose self-interest rules their every action. They conform to standards of society and accept its values. They function well in the Army, in politics and in the Church. The distinction between the lambs and buffaloes has been in evidence since the earliest works. The character of Frau Francke is a good example of the *Büffel* and Käte Bogner is a good example of the *Lämmer.* An illustration

---

[55]Ziolkowski, "Albert Camus and Heinrich Böll," p. 289.

[56]Karl Migner, "Heinrich Böll," in *Deutsche Literatur in der Gegenwart in Einzeldarstellungen,* ed. Dietrich Weber (Stuttgart: Kröner, 1976), p.207.

[57] From Hölderlin's poem "Wie wenn am Feiertag" in the edition by Norbert von Hellingrath.

[58]Reid, *Heinrich Böll. Withdrawal and Re-Emergence,* p.53.

of a character who has experienced both worlds is Walter Fendrich (*Das Brot der frühen Jahre*). He begins as a *Büffel* by accepting the life style of Ulla's father and by being primarily interested in material security. Upon meeting Hedwig Muller, he is drawn to the side of the *Lämmer*. His true nature returns to him when he leaves the materialistic restorative society behind. This redemption, as has been noted, occurs through the intervention of a woman.

This same type of female figure with redemptive powers is seen in the character of Edith Fähmel in *Billard um halbzehn*. She is depicted by Böll as the lamb *par excellence*. Like Käte Bogner, she is strong in her religious faith and a good mother and wife. She is described as a pure and innocent, almost virginal person. So much so that during sexual intercourse her husband has "das merkwürdige Gefuhl, sie wieder einmal geschändet zu haben."[59] Like Hedwig and Walter (*Das Brot der frühen Jahre*), the marriage of Robert and Edith at first is not sanctioned by the Church. Both couples view the ritual as a mere formality, and thus voice their protest against society that places more value on a rite than on substance.

Edith, like Böll's women figures before her, becomes a victim of the war. Her influence does not die with her however. As a lamb, she brings Heinrich, her father-in-law, a new feeling of religion: "als sie bei uns lebte, konnte ich seinen (Gottes) Namen wieder denken, ohne zu erröten, konnte den Namen beten" (p. 202-203). She teaches him to pray again, and to realize the dichotomy that exists between the *Lämmer* and the *Büffel*, causing him to question his position and to reevaluate his goals. This is reminiscent of the influence Hedwig wields on Walter, the difference being that Walter rejects the life of the *Büffel* totally, and becomes a *Lamm*. Heinrich has led a dual life for most of his life. He partakes in the

---

[59]Heinrich Böll, *Billard um halbzehn, Ansichten eines Clowns, Ende einer Dienstfahrt* (Cologne: Kiepenheuer and Witsch, 1974), p.107.

Sakrament des Büffels in that he enjoys the material gains and power and prestige that society affords him, yet he feels *ennui* and boredom with the status quo. This dualism within Heinrich is seen in the two sons he sires: Otto, the Nazi adherent, who dies fighting for the Nazi cause, and Robert, who withdraws from society altogether, eventually communicating with the outside world only through correspondence. In describing Edith, Heinrich says: "ich konnte nie glauben, daß sie einen Vater, eine Mutter gehabt hat--einen Bruder. Sie war eine *Botin des Königs* (p.130). Here Böll directly calls Edith an *Engel*, in the sense that she brings "Boten der Hoffnung . . . die der Vernichtung widersteht."[60] Like Käte, she views her sorrows as the will of God and is able to endure the oppression of the *Büffel* because of her religious convictions.

Indeed the figure of Edith is reincarnated in the character of Hugo in the next generation. Like Edith, he is a representative of the lamb. Hugo even resembles Edith in his smile: "Ich habe es gesehen . . . auf dem Gesicht eines Hotelboys, der Hugo heißt" (p.131). In the concluding chapter Robert adopts Hugo, symbolizing thus the transcendence of Edith's death and her reincarnation in Hugo, a positive sign of hope on the part of Böll.

Edith, like Ilona, Käte Bogner and *das Mädchen* before her, is depicted as a very passive, religious, and domestic individual. They all fulfill the very traditional role relegated to woman. They support and nourish both physically and spiritually their families, especially their men. Edith's innocent and virginal nature is stressed by strong biblical overtones in her language: "Ich erwarte ein Kind. Der Herr hat mich gesegnet" (p.99). Much like her daughter-in-law Edith, Johanna is also depicted as pure and innocent. There is however, one important difference in the character of Johanna, something that has not been seen in Böll's previous women figures. Her opposition to the *Büffel* is active and aggressive. This

---

[60] Plard, p.74.

44

is a significant development in Böll's depiction of women, and the culmination of this development will be seen in the latest of Böll's works, *Die verlorene Ehre der Katharina Blum.*

Johanna actively looks for her son Robert when he is stopped by the Nazis. During the war she has more than enough food for her family, she does not spoil her own children, but allows them only enough to satisfy their needs. The rest she gives to the poor, with whom she feels spiritually akin and compelled to suffer:

> Sie schenkte alles weg, was sie extra bekam, und sie
> bekam viel . . . Butter in Fässern, Honig in Krügen . . .
> aber sie aß nichts davon und gab ihren Kindern nichts
> davon . . . (p.157).

Johanna is committed to a mental institution to protect her from the Nazis, as her resoluteness to speak her mind will surely bring her death. She decides to stay there after the war in her own words "in der inneren Emigration" (p.121). Like Fred Bogner and Nella Bach, she initially retreats within herself because of her inability to acknowledge this materialistic society that has failed to heed Christ's plea "weide meine Lämmer."

On September 6th Johanna decides to leave the institution to carry out a plan of revenge on the *Büffel,* the oppressors of society. She acquires a gun and attempts to assassinate the Cabinet Minister, who is in town on the occasion of a war memorial service. She fails in her attempt, but does wound him. It is important to note that her shot is not aimed at her personal enemy, Nettlinger, but at a minister of the government, "the demagogue of the new 'democratic' Germany."[61] Johanna is one of the few active lambs, willing to risk exile or death to voice her protest against the *Büffel.* This shot fired by Johanna signals the end of withdrawal from

---

[61]Ziolkowski, "Albert Camus and Heinrich Böll," p.290.

reality on her part.

Heinrich's daily observance year after year of breakfast at Kröner's Café signifies the boredom and complacency which he feels. Böll often makes use of the restaurant and hotel as a microcosm of society at large.[62] A place where formality is the order of the day and where one neatly regulates everything through money. It offers as much an escape to Heinrich as the insane asylum offers Johanna.[63] Café Kröner, is depicted as a negative place, a fashionable place occupied by those who have prospered from Germany's *Wirtschaftswunder*. But Heinrich cancels this breakfast ritual in the Café Kröner, after his wife's assassination attempt, which seems to pull him out of the past and into the present. Böll thus continues his advocation of a return to an active participation in life.

Robert Fähmel, like his mother, has taken the oath of the *Lämmer* not to participate in the "Sakrament des Büffels." He does not partake of the sacrament of the lamb, but as his mother explains:

> der ist deutsch, liest Hölderlin, hat nie vom Sakrament
> des Büffels gekostet, er ist vom Adel, kein Lamm, sondern
> ein Hirte (p.119).

He and his friend Ferdi Pögulski attempt to assassinate a high ranking Nazi official. His friend is hanged for this attempted assassination and Robert, after a period of exile in Holland, joins the army and destroys dwellings and churches of those he knows have participated in the *Sakrament des Büffels*. Among the destroyed buildings is the Abbey of St.Anthony, built by his father. The monks of the Abbey had held a torch-lit

---

[62]Reid, *Heinrich Böll: Withdrawal and Re-Emergence*, p.48.

[63]Böll places a great deal of significance on eating, as is evidenced in the title alone of one of his novels *Das Brot der frühen Jahre*. Walter Fendrich decides to leave his past behind in the Café Joos. A scene in the small café in *Und sagte kein einziges Wort*, run by *das Mädchen*, marks a decisive turning point for Käte and Fred.

procession to greet the Nazis and hence Robert feels justified as the shepherd, who is looking out for his sheep, in destroying it. It was, as Robert states: "ein Denkmal für die Lämmer, die niemand geweidet hatte" (p.53).[64]

When Robert's wife Edith becomes a war casualty, Robert totally withdraws from society. Much like Nella Bach, he cannot forget the past and remarry to begin a new life. "He denies himself the act of recreating . . . both (Nella and Robert) choose frozen sterility and activities as near to utter meaninglessness as possible."[65] He gives up his profession to become a statistician, carrying on his business exclusively through correspondence. Every morning at 9:30 he plays billiards at the Prinz Heinrich Hotel.[66] The only person with whom he has any dealings is Hugo, the bellboy. And at the end of the novel, Robert adopts Hugo as his son, perhaps a sign that like his mother and father, he has at last decided to put the past behind him and begin anew. As Hugo is portrayed as a reincarnated Edith, a woman once more figures in this change.

In *Ansichten eines Clowns*, much as the abbey in *Billard um halbzehn*,

---

[64]It is interesting to note how Böll's regard for the monastary has undergone a radical change. In *Nicht nur zur Weihnachtszeit*, Böll offered the monastary as an "alternative society" to the real world, a refuge from a bureaucratic and materialistic world. Ilona of *Wo warst du, Adam?* had left the convent in order to fulfill her desire for a family of her own. She is killed as a result in the hostile world. In *Und sagte kein einziges Wort* the retarded boy is drawn to the Gregorian chants sung by the monks, casting the idea of such a retreat in a positive light. In *Haus ohne Hüter*, Albert enjoys the church of the nuns, although the nun Bolda leaves the convent to return to the world. Here, in *Billard um halbzehn*, the monks actively participate in a Nazi torch-lit procession. This development culminates when the nun Klementina is persuaded to leave the convent, ending altogether Böll's advocation of a retreat or refuge from the world.

[65]Walter H. Sokel, "Perspective and Dualism in the Novels of Böll," in *The Contemporary Novel in German: A Symposium*, ed. Robert R. Heitner (Austin: U. of Texas, Press, 1967), p.17.

[66]The hotel, like Cafe Kröner, represents the empty controlled life without a family.

the Catholic seminary where Hans Schnier's brother Leo is studying to become a priest is a negative symbol. The only priest who shows virtues of brotherhood and kindness is considered a fool by his fellow seminarians. Withdrawal can no longer be condoned by Böll, it must end.

The novel itself encompasses one day, beginning in the late afternoon and ending about 9:00 at night. The point of view of the novel is however a single first person narrative. Through a series of flashbacks into his past, the reader becomes well acquainted with Hans Schnier, "ich bin ein Clown . . . und sammle Augenblicke."[67] It is these moments that the reader experiences.

Hans Schnier is a twenty-seven year old professional clown. He has rejected his social background and his rich, prestigious family. He has been traveling for the last five years around Germany in an attempt to tell "durch Schminke und Maske hindurch die ungeschminktesten Wahrheiten."[68] Although he has rejected the protestant church of his family, Hans is moved by Catholic liturgical hymns, which he loves to sing in the bathtub. His father is a wealthy and influential industrialist and his mother a hypocrite depicted much in the same vein as Frau Francke in *Und sagte kein einziges Wort*. Hans has lost his sister Henriette in the war, as a result of the stupidity of his mother. She encouraged Henriette to join the Nazi cause and work for the anti-aircraft company in the last stages of the war, at which time she becomes a war fatality.

Hans' companion for the last five years has been a young Catholic girl, Marie Derkum. In a fashion characteristic of many Böll pairs, they have been living together as man and wife without benefit of the formal marriage ritual. Hans sees love as the basis of marriage and thus regards himself as married, and is quite faithful to Marie. He sees no need for

---

[67]Heinrich Böll, *Ansichten eines Clowns* (Munich: Deutscher Taschenbuch Verlag, 1963), p.204.

[68]Pickar, p.27.

empty and meaningless church rituals. As the novel opens, however, Marie has left Hans to marry another man. Hans cannot perform now that he has lost Marie, begins to drink, and his last performance on stage is a disaster. He returns to Bonn, where he has an apartment. At this point the action begins. Hans, in an attempt to seek help, money and consolation, calls several people on the telephone and meets with his father. His father attempts to convince him to study mime, a "true art," in his opinion, an undertaking he is most willing to finance. Hans cannot leave his ideals by the wayside, being the individualist and non-conformist that he is, and ends up begging in the streets for money, while he plays the guitar and sings satirical political songs.

Like Robert Fähmel before him, Hans Schnier withdraws from a society whose ideals and morality he cannot condone. Much like Johanna Fähmel, who can only survive in an insane asylum, Hans hides behind a mask. He becomes a clown, viewing the world from the outside looking in. This is reminiscent of Günter Grass' dwarf, Oskar Matzerath, whose insights into society and its ills are prophetic and honest. Johanna Fähmel plays a game of pretence. She imagines she is imprisoned in a magic castle: "Schloß, in das ich verwünscht bin . . . nur durch riesige Leitern ist die Welt erreichbar" (p.104). She asks her husband and son to indulge her in this game, which they do. Hans, however, is not playing at being a clown. It is his profession, his way of life. He cannot distinguish between what is real and what is play, resulting in total alienation:

> Ich kann einen Blinden so gut spielen, das man glaubt, ich
> wäre blind. Ich kam mir auch blind vor, vielleicht würde
> ich blind bleiben (p.154).

He has no concept of time, be it present or past, hence his "Augenblicke" lack any systematic chronological order, and blend together.

The action of the novel depicts Schnier's suffering "at the hands of the Catholics the fate that his older sister had suffered at the hands of the

49

Nazis in the Bonn of 1945."[69]   Marie could also be viewed as Henriette's
Doppelgestalt.[70]   Marie leaves Hans through the prodding of several
Church intellectuals, much as Henriette left her family because of her
mother's insistence that she join the Nazi war cause. Both women become
permanently separated from Hans, who loves them both. Henriette
possesses a unique talent, she was able to free herself totally from reality
for short periods of time. Bernath feels that Hans' choice of careers, or
art, is an imitation of Henriette's unique talent:

> Hans Schniers Kunst ist nichts anderes als eine
> eigenartige, zeitlich ausgedehnte Wiederholung der
> Fähigkeit von Henriette . . . das Clown-Sein: die
> bewußte Entpersönlichung, das Leer-Werden, die
> Selbstentfremdung, wird Hans Schniers einzige
> Daseinsform.[71]

With Marie at his side he is able to perform his art, but after she is gone,
his symbolic death occurs on stage. As the curtain comes down, he
visualizes it as a funeral shroud. His painted mask becomes a death mask.
Unlike Böll's earlier "Liebe im Krieg" story, *Der Zug war pünktlich*, whose
utopian ending signified a final unification of the lovers in the hereafter,
the feeling here is one of total alienation. Bernath suggests that Böll
regards the restorative society as the "'schlimmste' Krieg, (der) nicht zu
Ende geht."[72] This would justify the ending and indicate a return to the
same motif with which Böll began, the "Liebe im Krieg."

At a very early age, Schnier rebelled against school, refused to take
tests and left school early to pursue a "brotlose Kunst" -- to be a clown. He

[69]Sokel, p.31.

[70]Bernath, pp.36-38.

[71]*Ibid.*, p.40.

[72]*Ibid.*, p.39.

rejects his bourgeois upbringing at home, refusing to become a cog in his father's business, where a good future could be secured for him. Like Fendrich, (*Das Brot der frühen Jahre*) he rejects the material gains of society so readily accessible to him. He cannot partake in the *Sakrament des Büffels*, for he would be compromising his individuality. Upon meeting Marie, both instinctively know that they are meant to be together. Like Hedwig, Marie yields to Hans without reservation. Marie attempts to fit Hans into the circle of Catholic intellectuals she knows, but in keeping with his hatred of categorization, Hans not only rejects them, he cannot tolerate their snobism, and they become the object of his attack. Hans has always detested labels such as bourgeois, Catholic, or comedian, for those classifications are general and not based on individual criteria: "By attaching national, political or ideological group-labels to individual people we blind ourselves to the reality of their human situation."[73] In his eyes, that is precisely the problem with the Church, it has become just one more pressure group in society, losing sight of individual needs. The circle of Catholic intellectuals that Böll depicts in this novel is typical in its lack of concern for the individual. They gather to discuss on one occasion "Armut in der Gesellschaft, in der wir leben." They begin to argue about what amount constitutes poverty. Instead of seeking practical means to help the poor, they discuss the problem in abstract academic terms. This elitism on the part of the Church is contrary to the principles upon which it was founded. This circle of Catholic intellectuals, which Marie often visits, convinces her to leave Hans and end their unsanctioned relationship. They approve of Hans' father, who has a mistress, but do not approve of the monogamous relationship between Marie and Hans. It is also suggested that the motivation for encouraging Marie to leave Hans was based on personal animosity. Hans suspects that one of the members of the group

---

[73]H. R. Klieneberger, "Heinrich Böll in *Ansichten eines Clowns*," in *German Life and Letters*, 19 (1965-66), p.16.

has intentions towards Marie, which indeed proves true. Soon after the split, Marie marries the well-known political, Catholic church leader Züpfner. Hans views this marriage as adultery, as he feels truly bound in love toward Marie.

As the novel opens the reader is presented with a picture of a broken man full of self-pity. The reason behind this man's unhappiness is quickly seen to be a woman. The questions arise whether she was justified in hurting this man and what her motivation might have been. In an attempt to answer these questions, the reader is restricted exclusively to Hans Schnier's narrative perspective, but the character portrayal of Marie becomes quite clear as past conversations unfold.

Marie's father, who was once active in politics, but is now viewed as a difficult, uncooperative man, is a shopkeeper, and is hardly making ends meet. When Hans goes to tell him about Marie and himself, he is somewhat angry, but he forgives Hans almost immediately. Hans asks him for money and Marie's father gives him what little he has:

> "Schenken Sie mir noch eine Schachtel Zigaretten," und er griff sofort hinter sich ins Regal und gab mir zwei Schachteln. Er weinte. Ich beugte much über die Theke und küsste ihn auf die Wange. Er ist der einzige Mann, den ich je geküsst habe" (p.257).

They reach a silent understanding, they know that they both share love for Marie. Love is a moral justification for Hans' actions and therefore the father knows he cannot object.

Marie was the center of Hans' existence. It is important to evaluate his comments about her, since they are the only source of our knowledge about her. When Hans describes Marie as "naiv, und sehr intelligent war sie nicht" (p.305), the reader is forced to question the validity of Schnier's evaluation. She was a good student in school, and much like Hedwig Muller, would have pursued a career and further education, had she not met Hans, for whom she abandoned her family and her education. She prefers cultural discussions to Hans' fascination with the game *Mensch ärgere dich nicht.*[74]   Hans is somewhat reminiscent here of Robert Fähmel, in that both choose games as close to utter meaninglessness and uselessness as possible. As the novel progresses, the reader is better able to identify with Marie, than with Hans Schnier himself.[75]   As the reader seeks to discover Marie's true nature, he goes beyond the first person monologue of Hans, and "draws upon material and insights inherent (there) in."[76]

It is interesting to note that Hans Schnier, although not satisfied with his life before he met Marie, did nothing actively to change it. He still lived at home with his family, despite his disapproval of them and what they represented. It is not until his consummation, "rebirth," with Marie, that he sets out to pursue his act as a clown. She, like Hedwig with Walter, kindles new life into his soul through love. He realizes he can no longer passively observe the wrongdoings of society and pursues a career in which he can express (even if it is a silent protest through mime) his discontent and perhaps make public his protest by refusing to participate in a materialistic society. In his choice of professions alone, "das Clown-Sein," Schnier voices a protest in indulging in a "brotlose Kunst." Marie is able to instill this courage in him. After her departure, he cannot proceed with his art and abandons it to become a beggar. In choosing to become a beggar in the streets, he will serve as a constant reminder to society that not all is well and happy in this time of materialistic wealth, a position of offense, not withdrawal.

---

[74]This is the game Böll himself loves to play with his children, indicating perhaps that his sentiments seem to lie with Hans Schnier, an innocent soul in conflict with the world around him.

[75]Pickar, p.31.

[76]*Ibid.,* p.31.

Marie is a positively drawn character, whose human failings and errings are understandable. She is not a very strong-willed person, and can be easily persuaded. She is different from Käte Bogner, in that she suffers in silence for a while, but then does leave Hans, characteristically, however, through the intervention of others.

It is in this novel in the character of Frau Schnier (Hans' mother) that Böll portrays his most unforgettable negative female character. After the war she became President of the Central Committee of Societies for the Reconciliation of Racial Differences. Like Frau Francke (*Und sagte kein einziges Wort*), she is an opportunist; both have committed unforgivable crimes against their fellow human beings (in Frau Schnier's case her own family) and reap rewards instead of admonishments from society. They have no principles and rather than follow their hearts, go with whatever ideology can bring them material rewards. Frau Schnier loses her son's respect early in his youth and her husband has sought the companionship of another woman.

Herbert Kalick is the male counterpart of Frau Schnier. He was a Hitler Youth leader, who accidentally killed a boy and nearly killed Hans. After the war he is a well-to-do businessman and politician and tries to win over Schnier's approval, but Hans detests him and can see through his shallow exterior.

In his depiction of the positive men figures in this novel, Böll makes it clear that they are by no means supermen, who easily overcome adversity. On the contrary, they are very unenergetic, nonconformist, compassionate individuals. Böll allows both Marie's father and Hans Schnier to cry and even kiss. Böll's positive female figures are innocent, naive, religious and compassionate. It is in this novel, *Ansichten eines Clowns*, that Böll reveals the following view of women:

> Eine Frau kann mit ihren Händen so viel ausdrücken oder
> vortäuschen, daß mir Männerhände immer wie

angeleimte Holzklötze vorkommen. Männerhände sind
Händedruckhände, Prügelhände, natürlich Schießhände
und Unterschrifthände. Drücken, prügeln, schießen, und
natürlich: arbeiten. Frauenhände sind schon fast keine
Hände mehr: ob sie Butter aufs Brot oder Haare aus der
Stirn streichen. Kein Theologe ist je auf die Idee
gekommen, über die Frauenhände im Evangelium zu
predigen: Veronika, Magdalena, Maria und Martha--
lauter Frauenhände im Evangelium, die Christus
Zärtlichkeiten erwiesen . . . Statt dessen predigen sie über
Gesetze, Ordnungsprinzipien, Kunst, Staat. Christus hat
sozusages privat fast nur mit Frauen Umgang gehabt.
Natürlich brauchte er Männer, weil sie wie Kalick ein
Verhältnis zur Macht haben, Sinn für Organisation und
den ganzen Unsinn. Er brauchte Männer so wie man bei
einem Umzug einfach Möbelpacker braucht, für die grobe
Arbeit, und Petrus und Johannes waren ja so
liebenswürdig, daß sie fast schon keine Männer mehr
waren, während Paulus so männlich war, wie es sich für
einen Römer geziemte. Wir bekamen zu Hause bei jeder
sich bietenden Gelegenheit aus der Bibel vorgelesen, weil
es in unserer Verwandtschaft von Pastoren wimmelt,
aber keiner hat je über die Frauen im Evangelium oder so
etwas Unfaßbares wie den ungerechten Mammon
gesprochen (pp. 202-203).

The images Böll uses to describe the female are "Butter aufs Brot
oder Haare aus der Stirn streichen." Both acts are gestures of love,
affection and compassion. Böll alludes to the fact that Christ, in his private
life, preferred the company of women over men. He refers especially to
four women who exhibited and were shown great compassion: Veronica,
Mary Magdalene, Mary and Martha. Böll's positive female characters
take on the qualities these women possessed. It is interesting to note Böll's
choice of Mary and Martha in his depiction of possible female figures.
Women, during the time of Jesus, were not allowed to learn the *Torah*; this
was a privilege open to men only. When Jesus would talk with women,
"the disciples marveled that he was talking with a woman." In the story of

Mary and Martha, as related in Luke 10:38-42, Martha complains to
Christ that Mary should be in the kitchen helping her serve, not out talking
to Him and leaving her to do the work by herself. Jesus replies "It is Mary
who has chosen the better part; it is not to be taken from her." Mary is
eager to learn from Him; lessons that were denied to other Jewish women.
The story of Mary and Martha seems to show the polarity between doing
and being. Martha is depicted as the tending, serving, nurturing one, the
female, whereas Mary is the disciple, apostle, leader and theologian, the
male. This story of the two sisters and Jesus makes clear His view of
women as "full intellectual human beings, persons who could believe and
explain that belief to others."[77] Women are able to function in the
intellectual realm and still retain their womanhood. There is, however, no
mention made of woman's role in the business and political realm. Several
of Böll's loving *Engel* characters were active in the intellectual realm:
Ilona had completed her *Staatsexamen* in German and music and was an
accomplished musician; Olina was a music student and fine pianist;
Hedwig Muller (*Das Brot der frühen Jahre*) and Marie Derkum (*Ansichten
eines Clowns*) were both pursuing higher education when they met the
men in their lives, but both abandoned this pursuit for their men. Böll is still
the traditionalist in his view of women as the loving, compassionate,
nurturing human beings. These qualities are glorified by Böll, and women
offer the only glimmer of hope and humanity in desolate times, such as
war. They are the only ones capable of self-sacrifice and service to fellow
mankind. Wartime is described by Böll as a world without women, a time
devoid of love and compassion. The two men Böll mentions in a positive
light in this quoted passage are Peter and John. He refers to them as being
so loving that they are almost no longer men. Men are those who shoot
guns, sign checks, and work. Christ needed men because they had a sense

---

[77]Rachel Conrad Wahlberg, *Jesus According To A Woman* (New York: Paulist
Press, 1975), pp.80-81.

for organization and a desire for power "und den ganzen Unsinn."

When women take over masculine roles, such as Bertha does in *Wie in schlechten Romanen*, they are depicted in a very negative light. When her husband describes her hands, "die Schecks unterschreiben," he becomes aware of his aversion toward her. Guided by her selfish ambition, she is unconcerned with her husband's own inner moral convictions. Frau Francke, in *Und sagte kein einziges Wort*, is guided by the same sense of selfishness and ambition.[78]

Whenever men take on the feminine qualities of love and compassion, they are depicted in a most positive light. The best example is perhaps Albert Muchow (*Haus ohne Hüter*) whose unselfish love for his fellow human being allows him, as a Christ figure, to save Wilma Brielach, a Mary Magdalene figure. Marie Derkum's father, (*Ansichten eines Clowns*) serves as another example of a man who has taken on female qualities, because of his generosity toward others. When Hans tells him about himself and Marie, the father weeps and Hans returns his affection by kissing him on the cheek. This is a very moving scene between two men sharing their emotions outwardly, a rare occurrence in Böll's depiction of men. Neither man has a sense of organization or desire for power and hence are regarded in the positive sense usually reserved for women.

The feeling of alienation Hans feels and his consequent withdrawal from reality is further developed in Böll's next two prose works *Entfernung von der Truppe* and *Ende einer Dienstfahrt*. The titles alone

---

[78]Böll's choice of names for the majority of his positive female characters seem to be of non-Germanic origin. The negative characters' names are all of Old German origin. Käte and Katharine from the Greek mean "pure one;" Johanna comes from the Hebrew meaning "God is gracious;" Edith comes from the Hebrew meaning bitter or bitterness. The negative characters Ulla and Bertha come from the Old German meaning "owner of an inherited estate" and "shining glorious one." It becomes apparent that Böll's choice of names was a deliberate one and offers a key to the nature of personality. This thesis also holds true for Böll's later choice of positive female names -- Leni, Margret, Rahel, Klementina and Katharina Blum.

project a feeling of resignation from life, or "das Weitergehen des Lebens."
Entfernung von der Truppe is the story of a young philology student, who
is drafted at the age of twenty one. He meets his best friend, *Engel*bert
Bechtold in the army and marries Engelbert's sister Hildegard. After he
has found this love with her, he deserts the army. He is arrested and sent
to the front. His wife, who has given birth to a daughter, is killed during
the war, as well as his best friend and now brother-in-law, Engelbert.
After the war he decides not to return to the world and chooses a self-
exile, refusing to participate in society. This is much like Nella Bach in
Haus ohne Hüter. His withdrawal is not just from the past, for he cannot
accept the present either. His philosophy rings: "Daß Menschwerdung
dann beginnt, wenn einer sich von der jeweiligen Truppe entfernt."[79] The
only contact he has with reality is through his three-year-old grandchild
Hildegard and his mother-in-law, who takes him in like a son. She labels
her own surviving son a *Miefer* and her daughter-in-law *eine überflüssige
Belästigung*, and says of her own husband: "wenn wir geschieden wären,
könnten wir nicht geschiederner sein" (p. 381). She often says to Wilhelm,
"du bist immer noch von der Truppe entfernt" (p. 381), and they have an
unspoken understanding of the meaning of these words.

The title *Ende einer Dienstfahrt* conveys the same tone of
resignation and withdrawal as *Entfernung von der Truppe*. It is the story
of a law-suit against a father and son, who are accused of burning an
army jeep in the fields in June, 1965. The burning as a protest against a
merciless economic system stands at the core of the story. The reactions on
the part of a myriad of people is recorded. It seems the only one who is
fully aware of the meaning of the Gruhls' protest is Grete Horn. She sees
this "Happening" as an opportunity to gain publicity and attention in the
political realm for the ailing and destructive economic system of the
country. She sums up the situation as follows:

---

[79]Böll, *Erzählungen 1950-1970*, p.381.

58

> (Sie) bezeichnete alle mit dem Fall Gruhl befaßten
> Männer, ihren eigenen einbegriffen als 'Schwachköpfe,'
> die nicht verstünden, welche Chance sich in der
> Möglichkeit verberge, diesem Fall Publicity zu
> verschaffen. "Stell dir vor," sagte sie ruhig, "alle
> Soldaten kämen auf die Idee, ihre Autos und Flugzeuge in
> Brand stecken." Aber diese laffen Sozialdemokraten,
> diese scheinheiligen Schwindler, sind ja noch bürgerlicher
> als die Bürger geworden (P. 444).

All others seem to de-emphasize the political significance of such a protest.
The case is hastily brought to trial in a village court and disposed of. The
Gruhls are reprimanded and given a minimal fine, to dismiss any chance of
further publicity. In this novel the theme of protest against society is no
longer couched in the acts of a single individual, but becomes a common
endeavor of father and son. In Böll's next novel, *Gruppenbild mit Dame*,
the protest outgrows even the institution of the family, and become a
group affair.

The women from Ilona and Olina to Wilma to Johanna Fähmel have
undergone a significant change. The war and its aftermath has forced a
reexamination of the woman's role. In these works Böll has recorded her
response to such trials. Some withdraw into the past, unable to participate
in what Böll calls "das Weitergehen des Lebens (Nella Bach)." Some feel
the need to reach out to others in an attempt to find a meaning in their
lives (Wilma Brielach).

In Böll's view, the time of material accumulation and wealth
(*Wirtschaftswunder*) is an extension of the totalitarian state that existed
under Hitler, underscored by man's lack of independence and individuality.
Those who refuse to participate in the scramble for prestige, position and
wealth, the *Lämmer*, fall prey to the *Büffel*. The innocent Edith is a
continuation of the *Engelfigur*, Böll has depicted in prior novels. She
possesses a deeply religious faith and confidence in God, which enables her

to rise above the persecution. Johanna withdraws from war society into an insane asylum. She suddenly chooses to end this withdrawal and actively voices her protest against the status quo by an assassination attempt on a cabinet minister. Her shot marks the beginning of an active opposition against the *Büffel*, the oppressors of society. Johanna's action marks a significant development in Böll's depiction of womanhood, the culmination which shall be seen in Katharina Blum.

Chapter Three

Gruppenbild mit Dame

Leni Pfeiffer, the female protagonist in *Gruppenbild mit Dame*, has much in common with the women who precede her. Like Käte Bogner she is the outsider in the hostile world of the *Wirtschaftswunder*. Like Edith Fähmel she is able to influence those around her, revealing the contrast between her own humanity and their materialistic ethos and indifference. Like Katharina Mirzowa and Hedwig Muller she acts out of an intuitive knowledge of what is right, without regard for *Ordnungsprinzipien*. To a degree unlike any of her predecessors, however, Leni possesses an erotic sensuality which lies at the very core of her nature; she is described as "ein verkanntes Genie der Sinnlichkeit" (p. 38).[1] It is precisely this generous sensuality that prevents her from fitting into the framework of an orderly world, making her an individualist. She does not withdraw from the world, as Käte before her, but perseveres and survives, remaining as Böll himself states, "fast unverletzt."[2]

The *Verfasser*, the assumed author, solicits statements from a myriad of individuals (*Zeugenaussagen*, p. 126) in order to comprehend the personality and nature of the heroine, Leni Pfeiffer. He compiles reports, facts, conversations and personal memories in an attempt to lend a documentary format to the novel. He conducts interviews with fifty-two informants who have had contact with her. The narrative perspective somewhat resembles the one Böll employed in *Ende einer Dienstfahrt*, in which a number of witnesses are called upon to offer their opinions about

---

[1] Heinrich Böll, *Gruppenbild mit Dame* (Köln: Kiepenheuer and Witsch, 1971), p. 33.

[2] Heinrich Böll/Dieter Wellershoff, *"Gruppenbild mit Dame*. Ein Tonbandinterview," *Akzente*, 18 (1971), p. 332.

the Gruhls' act of turning an army jeep. Much like the Gruhls, Leni survives the events relatively unscathed. In *Gruppenbild mit Dame*, however, the *Erzählzeit* stretches from 1890-1971, whereas *Ende einer Dienstfahrt* concerns itself with only a few days. It is interesting to note that as the number of narrators has increased from two in *Und sagte kein einziges Wort* to fifty-two in *Gruppenbild mit Dame*, the *Erzählzeit* has expanded in direct proportion. In order to avoid "literizing" this accumulated material, the *Verf.* includes "authentic" documentation, "Auszüge aus Protokollen, Prozeßakten, die ich als Collage verwendete."[3] Leni herself is described as reticent and taciturn (*wortkarg*). All of her direct comments are recorded on two and a half pages in the novel (p. 309-311). As the informants describe Leni and their contact with her, the reader gains a great deal of information about the informants themselves and what effect their contact with Leni had on their lives. In Böll's own words their *Mitmenschlichkeit* is in question and they are tested through Leni's presence,[4] hence the title *Gruppenbild mit Dame*. These informants represent many social classes, ages and races, thus a diversified and varied picture of Leni as well as the informants is gained. The witnesses to Leni's forty years comprise a sort of "stained glass-window,"[5] or mosaic of Leni. At the same time Böll is able to portray a variety of reactions to war and

---

[3]*Ibid.*, p. 337. As Zioloski notes, these novels share the following characteristics: the life of the main character is pieced together through letters, interviews, transcripts and photos; the narrator is so filled with compassion for the main character that his stance is no longer an objective one; the position of the narrator to the subject matter is made totally clear at the beginning of the novel. (Theodore Ziolwoski, "Typologie und 'Einfache Form' in *Gruppenbild mit Dame*," ed. Renate Matthaei (Cologne: Kiepenheuer & Witsch, 1975), p. 131-132. The documentary format is seen in other numerous contemporary works: Nossacks' *Der Fall D'Arthez* (1968), Uwe Johnson's *Das dritte Buch über Achim* (1961), Christa Wolf's *Nachdenken über Christa T.* (1968), Siegfried Lenz' *Daz Vorbild* (1973).

[4]Deschner, p. 12.

[5]Melvin Maddocks, "Bölls Song of Innocence," *Atlantic Monthly* (July, 1973), p. 96.

restoration, and simultaneously give a panoramic and very human view of the years from 1890 to 1971.

By choosing the abbreviation *Verf.*, Böll attempts to lend objectivity to the narrator's findings. As the novel unfolds, it quickly becomes obvious that the *Verf.*'s feelings and views of Leni are anything but objective, although he assures us that his "Ermittlungen" are completely "faktenabhängig" (p. 322). He states at the beginning of the novel that he is "in Leni verliebt (p. 38)," although he will only have had contact with her twice by the close of the novel and those meetings are to be brief. He becomes increasingly involved in the action of the story, evolving from a reporter to a story teller until finally he is one of the characters in the novel itself. Why is the narrator so concerned with finding out all there is to know about Leni Pfeiffer? He claims to undertake this "unermüdliche Recherchierarbeit (p. 370)" only "um sich sachlich zu informieren (p. 377)" and purely "im Dienst der Wahrheit" (p. 342):

> Die Wahrheit über Leni Pfeiffer ist lebensnotwendig im Sinne der Überwindung des Nur-Vegetierens--mag es sich auch in konfortablem Interieur abspielen--im Sinne der Aufhebung des Ausgeliefertseins an eine Rolle als Objekt der Ausbeutung und Konsument. Es geht um die Wahrheit über einen Menschen, der in seinem exemplarisch zu verstehenden Dasein, in der Ablehnung des weithin für normal Gehaltenen, normal ist, der eine unveräußerlich humanistische Position vertritt.[6]

The narrator assures us that he is "weder von einer irdischen, noch von einer überirdischen Instanz gegeben, er sei existentiell" (p. 337). To fully answer the question of the narrator's motivation, it is necessary to

---

[6]Hans Joachim Bernhard, "Es gibt sie nicht, und es gibt sie. Zur Stellung der Hauptfigur in der epischen Konzeption des Romans *Gruppenbild mit Dame*," in *Die subversive Madonna*, ed. Renate Matthaei (Köln: Kiepenheuer un Witsch, 1975), p. 65.

return to what Böll said about the artist in *Ansichten eines Clowns*: "daß ein Künstler gar nicht anders kann als machen, was er macht" (p. 112). He feels an irrational need to simply do what he feels he must do. The *Verf.* must observe his surroundings and then report on them critically. An artist is committed to do this, for being an artist implies a binding obligation to society. In *Gruppenbild mit Dame*, the *Verf.* feels he must investigate Leni's life in order to reveal all that is wrong with society, but more importantly, to reveal how das *Menschsein* is still a possibility in this society. In his interview with Wellershoff, Böll revealed that a key word in *Gruppenbild mit Dame* is "Abfall und die Abfälligkeit der Gesellschaft."[7]

Leni and her commune of friends and *Gastarbeiter* are depicted as outsiders. Most of them, including her son Lev, are employed as *Müllfahrkutscher*. They are ironically regarded as *Untermenschen* or *Abfall*, because they are employed in a menial job -- keeping the city clean. Böll, in an interview with H. L. Arnold, makes his position clear by posing the following rhetorical question:

> Warum soll nicht der Sohn eines Universitätsprofessors, der das Abitur hat zur Müllabfuhr gehen, verstehen Sie, die ist notwendig, die ist ja fast notwendiger als die Universität.[8]

Leni Pfeiffer is Böll's first central female figure in a novel. She has been hailed by critics as "wohl die menschlichste Person, die Böll je gezeichnet hat."[9] "eine neue Dimension des Menschlichen, vielleicht ein neuer Mensch."[10] It becomes obvious from these accolades, that Böll has

---

[7]Böll/Weelershoff, p. 339.

[8]Im *Gespräch: Heinrich Böll mit Heinz Ludwig Arnold*, Edition *Text und Kritik* (Munich: Richard Boorberg Verlag, 1971), p. 59.

[9]Heinz Ludwig Arnold, "Heinrich Böll's Roman *Gruppenbild mit Dame*," p. 59.

[10]Rudolf Hartung, "Heinrich Böll/*Gruppenbild mit Dame*," in *Neue Rundschau,* (1971), p. 757.

shifted his emphasis from one of protest against one cause or another to a concentration on a depiction of a person who has survived her personal tragedies and sufferings with her *Nächstenliebe* and *Mitmenschlichkeit* intact. Böll has dealt with this type of figure before in the character of *das Mädchen* in *Und sagte kein einziges Wort*, but she was a secondary and ultimately passive figure. *Das Mädchen* has moved from the periphery of the novel to become the central character in the form of Leni Pfeiffer.

Böll opens the novel with a very precise physical description of Leni and a quick summary of the major events of her life. As in *Billard um halbzehn*, the information is provided by outsiders whose assessment of Leni is severe and abusive. She is labeled "mieses Stück," "ausgediente Matratze," "Schlampe," "Kommunistenhure," "Rußenliebchen," and "dumme Pute" by her neighbors (p. 33). The task of the *Verf.* lies in revealing Leni for what she really is, "eine schweigsame und verschwiegene, stolze, reuelose Person (p. 237)," "nicht verbittert," "müßig" and "rheinisch."

Leni is a very interesting combination of the sensual and pure/innocent.[11] Her name alone immediately attests to this fact, Helena Maria, the beautiful/sensual in combination with the innocent/religious: "Sie hätte als Heilige (auch Magdalena) in einem Mysterienspiel auftreten, als Reklame für Hautcreme verwendet werden, möglicherweise sogar in Filmen eine Rolle spielen können" (p. 51). Her nature reveals an harmonious combination of two characteristics usually considered irreconcilable. The *Verf.* acknowledges this when he refers to her as "die irdisch-materialistische menschlichhimmlische Leni."

Ralph Ley likens Leni to Bernini's Ecstasy of St. Theresa: "this Baroque masterpiece combines the extremes of mystic devotion and

---

[11]Pickar, p. 33.

sparkling sensuality to the point of orgasm inherent in Leni's makeup.[12]

Her sensual nature is even revealed in her daily breakfast ritual. She goes to the bakery every day to get fresh bread rolls, "den größten Wert legt Leni auf die frischen Brötchen" (p. 11). She gathers every crumb and consumes it as if it were a communion host. As a young girl she could hardly wait for the time she could at last partake in the Holy Communion, but when she receives it, her first instinct is to want to expel it: "Was war das für ein Brot, das man ihr gab . . . und wo, wo verflucht noch einmal blieb der Wein" (p. 33). It is dry and tasteless and does not at all resemble bread. Her religion teacher is so outraged by her impatience to receive communion and then her startling response, that he labels her behavior "kriminell" and holds her back for two years. Her sensual nature, her concreteness does not comprehend ritual alone, there must be substance. Her sensuous consumption of fresh bread becomes her substitute host.

The walls of her apartment are filled with paintings of human organs; Leni loves the human form and is not embarrassed by it. She is presently reproducing a cross-section of one layer of a nun's retina, painting 6,000,000 cones and 100,000,000 rods in detail. Geoffrey Wolff suggests that the *Verf.* is essentially doing the same thing for Leni's life.[13]

Leni's first erotic experience discloses her joint sensual and religious nature. On one beautiful summer day, at the age of sixteen, Leni lay in a field of heather, "ausgestreckt und ganz hingegeben" (p. 29). She experiences a feeling similar to orgasm and says she would not have been surprised to find herself pregnant, because at that moment she could fully understand the virgin birth of Christ.

Much as she awaited her first communion, Leni anxiously anticipates her first sexual encounter. She meets a young architect from

---

[12]Ralph Ley, "Compassion, Catholicism and Communism: Reflecions on Böll's *Gruppenbild mit Dame*," *University of Dayton Review* 10, ii: p. 31.

[13]Geoffery Wolff, "Still Life," in *Time*, May 18, 1973, p. 99.

her father's office and consents to a romantic rendezvous for the weekend. Nothing comes of it however, for when she dances with him, she immediately recognizes "der 'Kerl' habe keine 'zärtlichen Hände'" (p. 53). Leni's criterion for a lover is purely a spontaneous attraction, an instinctive feeling upon which she acts without hesitation.

It is interesting to note the significance Böll attaches to hands in his works. In *Ansichten eines Clowns*, he used hands to express the differences between men and women. Hands take on a meaning of unity among Leni's followers. This follows the traditional interpretation of two joined hands to signify a "mystic marriage . . . solidarity in the face of danger."[14] The members of Leni's group hold hands frequently; "Diese Händchenhalterei war so ansteckend, daß schließlich auch K. dazu überging, des Verf. Hand zu halten, so, also fühle sie ihm ständig den Puls" (p. 371). Leni, in joining hands with the architect, does not feel the spontaneity of love she had anticipated and immediately retreats.

The second man for whom she feels an attraction is her cousin Erhard Schweigert, who is too shy[15] to approach Leni, but "sie hätte ihn erhört, wenn er Erhöhung gebeten hätte" (p. 76). He is later executed along with Leni's brother Heinrich for desertion during the war. Her first sexual encounter finally comes with Alois Pfeiffer, an officer in the army. The narrator attributes Leni's act to the fact that she simply forgot herself. He labels the act "nicht einen moralischen, eher . . . einen existentiellen Fehltritt" (p. 120). His last name, Pfeiffer is reminiscent of the musical instrument of the pied piper, and he lures Leni through his dance into this sexual encounter.[16] She is very displeased with Alois' insensitivity and

---

[14]Cirlot, p. 131.

[15]Reid points out that the name Schweigert "reminds us of the important role played by silence in Böll's early works (*Und sagte kein einziges Wort, Doctor Murkes gesammeltes Schweigen*) in contradiction to the inflation of the language in contemporary society" (p. 582).

describes the experience as "unbeschreiblich peinlich" (p. 12), but for reasons of the family's *Ehre*, consents to marry him.

Leni refuses to wear white at her wedding. She later confided to Margret that Alois had forced her to fulfill her marital duties in the laundry room an hour before his departure for military duty. Leni reacts to the concept of *Pflicht* much like Schmölder in *Entfernung von der Truppe*. It detracts from the spontaneity and instills in her a sense of forced obligation, not love. When she is informed of his death three days after the marriage, she simply says he was "für mich gestorben bevor er tot war" (p. 125). She puts his picture *pflichtgemäß*, next to her photos of her brother Heinrich and her cousin Erhard Schweigert, but already removes it at the end of 1942. Leni's long awaited *Heidekrauterlebnis* finally finds reality in Boris Lvovich Koltovsky, a Russian prisoner of war. Leni meets him in the wreath shop where she is employed as a wreath maker (1944). Their encounter could not have come at a worse time or under worse conditions. As with Olina and Andreas (*Der Zug war pünktlich*) and Ilona and Feinhals (*Wo warst du, Adam?*), they are very unlikely lovers, and their choice of each other expresses their objection to a moral code forced upon them during the war. Like Olina and Ilona, Boris is considered the enemy, and friendship with him could mean death for both of them. This situation is typical for Böll, whose aim was to depict "eine Liebe zwischen Mann und Frau oder Frau und Mann in eine möglichst schwierige, heikle, politisch, sozial und äußerlich also durch die äusseren Einwirkungen des Krieges schwierige Situation."[17] Böll has chosen for Leni's lover what would be considered in wartime as the "zweitunterste Stufe Mensch nach der Nazi-Ideologie . . . den Untermenschen--Sowjetsoldat."[18] This episode is not

---

[16]Ingeborg L. Carlson, "Heinrich Böll's *Gruppenbild mit Dame* als frohe Botschaft der Weltverbindung," *University of Dayton Review*, ii (1975), p. 56.

[17]Böll/Wellershoff, p. 337.

[18]*Ibid.*, p. 338.

only central to Leni's life, but it comprises the core of the novel. When questioned about the *Gruppenbild mit Dame*, Böll repeats: "Wie meistens, wollte ich im Grund auch nur eine Liebesgeschichte schreiben."[19]

Leni's meeting with Boris is dubbed by the *Verf.* as "Lenis Geburt oder Wiedergeburt." The first day at work, Leni offers Boris a cup of her own coffee, "das war für die Leni eine Selbstverständlichkeit, jemand, der weder ne Tasse noch Kaffee hatte, eine Tasse Kaffee anzubieten" (p. 184). She had no idea what kind of political repercussions this could have, "Leni wußte immer erst, was sie tat, wenn sie es tat" (p. 190). As woman, according to Böll, she is simply following her natural kindness. When Kremp, a Nazi adherent and fellow worker of Leni's, throws his artificial leg at the cup, a long silence ensues, during which time Leni rinses out the cup "als wärs ein heiliger Kelch" (p. 185), dries it with utmost care and pours a second cup for him. Through this act of kindness, motivated by her "reine naive Menschlichkeit" (p. 187), "wurde (Boris) einfach durch Lenis mutige Tat zum Menschen gemacht, zum Menschen erklärt" (p. 187).

This scene between Leni and Boris is almost an exact repetition of the scene between Wilma and Albert on the stairs in *Haus ohne Hüter*. Albert is able to offer Wilma a "Glanz der Hoffnung" (p. 302) for a better life. The *Blick* they exchange is described in detail, much as the *Tausendstelsekunde* is discussed by the witnesses, who disagree on the duration of silence that ensued. It is interesting to note that the roles of men and women have been reversed. Albert's "Verheißung," a passive glance between two people, becomes an active act, as Leni offers Boris her "chalice of humanity." The male artist then (Albert) has served as the prototype for Böll's later women figures. Everyone in the group is affected by her warm display of humanity and the incident is vividly recalled by all the informants, down to the length of the silence after Kremp's protest. This time Leni simply takes the initiative, rather than letting it escape her again, as it had with Erhard.

---

[19]*Ibid.*, p. 337.

She places her left hand on his right, "es ging durch ihn, obwohl es nur ganz kurz dauerte, es ging durch ihr wien elektrischer Schlag" (p. 191). This *Handauflegung* marks the beginning of love between Boris and Leni. Böll appropriately chooses the joining of two hands to symbolize their mystical marriage. The transcendental side of Leni's nature is once more made clear, this time through the act of grace she initiates. This is all carried out in secret, and they find an appropriate love grotto in the catacombs of the graveyard, situated next to the wreath factory. In discussing her sexual experience with Margret, Leni says it was better than the *Heidekrauterlebnis*. The only time they are able to be together is during the air raids. Leni soon finds herself with child and she and Boris lead an "idyllic" existence among the catacombs.

Numerous religious allusions become obvious upon careful analysis of Leni's life, especially her sensual experiences stressing her unique combination of the religious and sensual. Her first sexual experience, the *Heidekrauterlebnis,* alludes to the Virgin birth which Leni is fully able to comprehend after her experience. The *Verf.* calls this experience by its theological name, *Seinserfüllung*, drawing a typological parallel to the Annunciation. It is interesting to note that Leni's birthday, August 17, 1922, falls on the Feast of the Assumption (p. 135). The only two prayers Leni knows are the *Lord's Prayer* and the *Ave Maria*. Her relationship with the Virgin Mary "steht . . . auf vertrautem Fuß, (Leni) empfängt sie auf dem Fernsehschirm fast täglich, jedesmal wieder überrascht, daß auch die Jungfrau eine Blondine ist" (p. 18). Leni is characterized as "wortkarg," this is in keeping with the description of the Virgin Mary in the Bible, she utters very little, if anything and her presence alone projects her innocence. The *Verf.* resorts to looking up the word *Unschuld* in a dictionary in an attempt to define Leni, "Leni . . . kann ohne diesen Begriff nicht verstanden werden" (p. 135). The *Verf.* mentions Leni's "religiöse Begabung" quite often and feels, "daß an ihr, an ihr vielleicht eine grosse Mystikerin zu endecken und zu entwickeln gewesen wäre" (p. 87).[20]

The love story between Boris and Leni brings forth a number of typological motifs. Boris is not a carpenter like Joseph, "aber wohl das moderne Gegenstück,"[21] a highway engineer. The first time Leni approaches Boris, they are working at the table in Pelzer's wreath shop. His reaction to her touch is described as "wien elektrischer Schlag." According to apocryphal literature, Joseph won Mary over as a bride through the miracle of the dead branch, which according to legend, began blooming when Joseph placed it on the altar of the temple. Like the dead branch brought to life again, Leni and Boris' love blossoms ironically in a wreath shop where the flowers are used to decorate the graves of the dead.

The *Verf.* goes to great length to determine that the child, Lev, must have been conceived on or about June 2, but he goes on to prove that there was no air raid on this day, indicating that Boris could not have been with Leni at that time. The reader is reminded of the *Heidekrauterlebnis*, which also took place on a June day, "wobei sich ein mystischer Zusammenhang zwischen den beiden Tagen einstellt."[22] The vault in the garden, *das Sowjetparadies in den Grüften*, is owned by a family with the name of Beauchamps, (in German Schönfeld), emphasizing again that Leni's bridal bed was made of heather.[23]

The *Handauflegung*, the laying-on-of-hands, is an act of benediction. In the Old Testament, Jacob blessed Joseph's sons by putting his hands upon their heads (Genesis 48: 14) and the Levites were consecrated to the priesthood through the laying on of hands (Numbers 8:

---

[20]These parallels are pinted our in Ziolowski, "Typologie und 'Einfache Form' in *Gruppenbild mit Dame*, pp. 126-27.

[21]Ziowolski, "Typologie und 'Einfache Form' in *Gruppenbild mit Dame*," p. 127.

[22]*Ibid.*, p. 128.

[23]Carlson, p. 54.

10, 20). In the New Testament, the apostles used the ceremony to impart the Holy Spirit to their converts (Acts 8: 19, 19). In Timothy II, Timothy is encouraged to "rekindle the Gift of God that is within you through the laying on-of-my-hands." The German translation of the biblical passage[24] is recalled by Böll's description of both Leni's and Boris' reaction to her laying on of hands: "entfache zulodernder Flamme die Gnadengabe Gottes, die dir durch meine Handauflegung innewohnt." And Margret describes Leni and Boris during the ceremony as being "sofort in Flammen" (p. 191). The *Handauflegung* follows the *Stunde der Tasse Kaffee* scene, structurally parallel to the biblical passage which defines love as the greatest of virtues (I Corinthians 13: 13): "NUN aber bleibt Glaube, Hoffnung, Liebe, diese drei; aber die Liebe ist die größte unter ihnen,"[25] and to the biblical passage encouraging the rekindling of spirituality through a laying-on-of-hands.[26] Leni is depicted as having the power to impart a renewal of faith to a community of believers as well as the ability to consecrate a person to the priesthood. She is able to acknowledge Boris as a *Mensch* through a laying-on-of-hands. When she offers Boris a cup of coffee, she offers him the "chalice" of humanity, love and brotherhood. After it is knocked from her hand by Kremp, she takes the utmost care in rinsing it with water and drying it, very reminiscent of the meticulous ceremony a priest partakes in after communion. Leni is able to establish a "neue Kirche" in the *Kranzbinderei*. The choice of the *Kranzbinderei* for the founding of the church is most appropriate here, for

---

[24]"daß du erweckest die Gabe Gottes, die in dir ist durch die Auflegung meiner Hände." *Die Bibel nach der Übersetzung Martin Luthers* (Stuttgart: Würtembergische Bibelanstalt, 1961).

[25]*Ibid.*, p. 229.

[26]Bernath, pp. 44-45.

in the figurative sense *Kranz* denotes innocence and virginity.[27] The phrase *im Kranz gehen* means to become a bride, which is precisely what Leni does, she becomes the bride of Christ in disseminating the new faith and Church to her group and simultaneously becomes the bride of Boris.

Leni's *Handauflegung* is extended to an act of healing. She is able to heal a wound by applying saliva to it: "Sie heilt nicht nur den Sowjetmenschen und ihren Sohn mit Speichel, durch bloßes Handauflegen versetzte sie den Sowjetmenschen in Glückseligkeit und beruhigte wie ihren Sohn" (p. 33). This is parallel to the function the *Handauflegung* served in the Gospel (Matthew 19: 13, 15) when Jesus blesses the children in this fashion. After a son is born of this union between Leni and Boris on March 2, 1945, they are described as the holy family:

> "Sie hätten sehen sollen, wie die beiden mit ihrem Söhnchen da hausten: wie die Heilige Familie. Er war doch nicht davon abzubringen, daß man eine Frau drei Monate nach der Entbindung nicht anfassen darf und auch vom sechsten Monat an nicht -- die haben doch ein halbes Jahr wie Maria und Joseph miteinander gelebt (p. 257).

Three months later Boris is sent to a labor camp in France where he is killed in a mining accident. Böll's theme of the forced separation of lovers is again recalled. Leni, before hearing of Boris' death, searches for her lover on a bicycle, riding all over Alsace. Johanna Fähmel, (Billard um halb zehn) before her commitment to the asylum, did the same when she heard that her son was missing. Leni returns home to raise her son Lev by herself, much like the Biblical Mary, for little mention is made of Joseph after the birth of Jesus.

Finally, the title of the novel itself, *Gruppenbild mit Dame* brings to

---

[27]*The New Cassell's German Dictionary*, (New York: Funk and Wagnalls, 1965), p. 277.

mind the *Notre Dame*, the Virgin Mary.[28]

Leni eventually falls in love again, this time with a Turkish *Gastarbeiter*, Mehmet, who lives in her building. She yields to his advances "weil sie es nicht erträgt, daß irgend jemand vor ihr kniet (daß sie selbst unfähig ist zu knien, gehört zu den vorauszusetzenden Eigenschaften)" (p. 10). In yielding, Leni joins a group of women Böll dubs *barmherzig*,

> eine Kategorie von Frauen, die nicht Huren und nicht Ehefrauen sind, die barmherzigen Frauen . . . eine Frau, die es nicht für Geld und nicht aus Leidenschaft für den Mann tut, nur aus Barmherzigkeit mit der männlichen Natur (*Ansichten eines Clowns*, p. 98-99).

Barmherzigkeit in this context is viewed as a combination of religious and sexual elements, "eine erotische Form der Caritas."[29]

Leni is expecting Mehmet's child at the close of the novel, an apparent happy end, signifying perhaps a new beginning for Leni, at the age of forty-eight. She is able to accept the Muslim religion, "da auch der Koran der Madonna einen Platz eingeräumt hat" (p. 365). Leni's acceptance of Mehmet, the Turkish *Gastarbeiter*, "macht sie zur allerbarmenden Allmutter in der archaischen Ur-Gemeinde eines klassenlosen und profitlosen Kommunalismus als Gegenmuster der heutigen Wohlstandsgesellschaft westlicher Prägung."[30] In a capitalistic society, where the profit motive rules the actions of its inhabitants, Böll offers Leni

---

[28]The Virgin Mary cult, which had its origin in the Middle Ages is well-documented by the ornate Gothic altarpieces depicting the Madonna and child. This offers a link between Böll's women figures and the role accorded them in the Middle Ages. This will be fully discussed in Chapter V.

[29]Bernd Balzer, "Einigkeit der Einzelgänger?" in *Die subversive Madonna*, ed. Renate Matthaei (Cologne: Kiepenheuer and Witsch, 1975) p. 19.

[30]Carlson, p. 60.

as an "Inbegriff einer humanistischen Gegenkraft."[31] Leni becomes a model who has not been influenced by the profit motive and its effects, but is an individual who acts out of her own moral integrity and generosity. This quality was very much in evidence in Böll's earlier female figures: *das Mädchen*, who, despite lean times, gave very generous servings at her café and in Johanna Fähmel who allowed her own children a minimal amount to eat in order to distribute the rest to the needy. The *Verf.* states that the second most important adjective describing Leni is "generös" (p. 235): "Sie war nun mal so herrlich proletarisch--vollkommen unfähig, das bürgerliche Profitdenken zu übernehmen oder gar zu praktizieren." When she becomes heir to her father's estate, she gives her father's cashmere vest to a "frierenden und darbenden Angehörigen einer für feindlich erklärten Macht" (p. 235), rather than sell it for a large monetary gain on the black market.

She borrowed money on her real estate property during the war to feed and provide for Boris and her friends, as well as to obtain false papers for Boris. The Hoysers, Leni's cousins, exploit this opportunity to gain control of the building. After the war Leni returns to this building to live and takes in several boarders. She has given the building a bad name by having *Gastarbeiter* live there and hence the Hoysers decide to evict her. They argue as follows:

> sie (Leni) sei ein Unmensch, denn ein gesundes Profit und Besitzstreben läge, und das sei von der Theologie nachgewiesen und werde sogar von marxistischen Philosophen immer mehr bejaht, in der Natur des Menschen (p. 348).

The perverse argument of the Hoysers about the immorality of those without property as opposed to the morality of money is an important part

---

[31]Bernhard, "Es gibt sie nicht, es gibt sie," p. 72.

of Böll's criticism of capitalism in its inability to respond to the Marxist challenge:

> Die westliche Welt -- die sich unter anderem auch christlich deklariert -- hat heute wie vor hundert Jahren, als Marx seine Theories entwickelte, keine andere Antwort bereit als die der Wohltätigkeit und der Unantastbarkeit des Privateigentum.[32]

The Hoysers insistence on accumulation for its own sake is indicated in their name (Häuser). They are contrasted with Leni's *Gemeinde* at the end of the novel, the *Leistungsverweigerer*. This contrast becomes evident in their names alone, each representing a totally different ideology: Hoyser-Häuser and Lev--Lvw (*Leistungsverweigerer*).

The *Verf.*'s sympathy for Leni's refusal to move from her present dwelling to what is called "better quarters" by the Hoysers, becomes obvious in the meeting between the Hoysers and the *Verf.* The older Hoyser cross-examines the *Verf.* as to his motivation for his interest in Leni. He becomes irate and aggressive with the *Verf.* and proceeds to rap him over the head with his cane. In the process he manages to tear a button and some material from the *Verf.*'s jacket. The younger Hoysers immediately offer to replace the jacket with a new and better one. The *Verf.* does not want a new one, for he is very fond of the old one. The Hoysers cannot comprehend why he would prefer the shabby jacket to a new expensive model. The *Verf.* responds:

> Kann man einem denn nicht glauben, daß man nur seine Jacke wiederhaben möchte, nichts weiter als seine Jacke . . . und gibt es nicht schließlich eine höhere Ökonomie, die es verbieten sollte, eine Jacke, die geflickt, kunstgestopft durchaus noch verwendbar ist und ihrem

---

[32]Heinrich Böll, "Karl Marx," in *Aufsätze, Kritiken, Reden* (Cologne: Kiepenheuer and Witsch, 1967), p. 87.

Träger Freude macht, einfach wegzuwerfen, nur, weil
man eine dicke Brieftasche hat und keinen Ärger haben
will? (p. 342-43)

The narrator is as attached to his jacket as Leni is to her *Bademantel,* in
which she wishes to be buried. Sentimental value cannot be bought, nor
can anything that is of emotional value. The *Verf.* experiences Leni's
feelings first hand and becomes ever more influenced by her.

The Hoysers see it as their duty to save Leni from herself and the
community of "subhumans" that gather around her. When they try to force
an eviction, Leni's community prevents the eviction by blocking the traffic
with their garbage trucks. They are successful in their endeavor and ban
together to maintain their idyllic existence.

Mehmet, like Boris, is regarded by some as an *Untermensch* and
Abfall. Contemporary German society has recreated the same hostile
environment that existed for Boris and Leni during the war. Like Boris and
Leni, Mehmet and Leni make an unlikely couple: Leni, who was chosen
"das deutscheste Mädel der Stadt" (p. 29) and Mehmet, a Muslim with a
wife and four children back home.

Trinität des Weiblichen

Böll addressed himself to the topic of woman and the traditional
thinking of the Church and society towards woman in a series of lectures
delivered in May, 1964, at the University of Frankfurt, where he served as
Poetik-Dozent. He is very critical of the Church's lack of explication of
texts concerning women in the Gospel. He reiterates this criticism in the
passages quoted from *Ansichten eines Clowns* on pages 202-203. He
defines the tension that exists in woman by three names: "Eva, Maria,
Magdalena, die sich nie rein, nie getrennt zeigen in der weiblichen
Natur."[33] He feels that today's literature deals with the Magdalenas and

---

[33]*Frankfurter Vorlesungen,* p. 100.

Evas, but has neglected the Maria aspect of the *Trinität des Weiblichen*. Woman, according to Böll, has repeatedly been treated as a *Lustspieleva* and a *Lustspielmagdalena*. Her virginal innocence has been ignored. Böll then undertakes the task to capture the threefold nature of woman in his heroine Leni Pfeiffer. The numerous parallels between Leni and the Virgin Mary have been outlined above, an examination of the other two components of Leni's nature is now in order.

Leni's physical good looks and sensual nature make her a temptation to all men around her: "Natürlich waren alle Männer hinter ihr her, irgendwie alle . . . aber getraut hat sich keiner . . . die war unnahbar" (p. 149). This attraction does not cease with her youth. The *Verf.* describes her as being capable of being a film star, or doing a commercial for skin cream. This attraction she holds for men carries with it an Eve-like carnal element. Walter Pelzer, the man for whom Leni worked during the war, comes to the following realization:

> die habe ich *begehrt,* seitdem ich sie zum erstenmal sah. . .
> verliebt war ich nicht in sie, das bin ich erst seit ich sie vor
> einer Woche widersah (p. 137).

Böll's conscious choice of the word *Sowjetparadies*[34] casts Leni and Boris in the role of Adam and Eve, a paradise from which they are uprooted by war and judgmental society, not a judgmental God. The genuine shamelessness Leni possesses is obvious from the paintings of genitals on her wall, recalling Eve before the Fall. Böll also includes an apple scene in the novel. The toilet is clogged by an apple core. Several unsuccessful attempts are made to clear the system. Leni simply plunges her arm in the

[34]The concept of paradise calls to mind the idea once again of a communal society, one without property. Böll's conscious use of the word Soviet is perhaps motivated by the fact that Böll is a very popular and widely read author in the Soviet Union (see Henry Glade in Bibliography). Here he takes a swipe at the prevailing anti-Russian feeling after the war.

filth and flings the apple away, saying: "unsere Dichter sind die mutigsten Kloreiniger gewesen" (p. 87). Here Böll makes reference to the characteristics that he feels unite the artist and the woman -- "sie müssen einfach machen, was sie machen müssen." The apple is symbolic of "earthly desires, or of indulgence in such desires."[35] The apple in the Book of Genesis in the Garden of Eden was not supposed to be eaten. It served as a warning against the exultation of materialistic desire. Nietzsche realized that the desire for knowledge, the intellect, is only an intermediate zone between earthly desire and pure spirituality.[36] Leni represents all three of these spheres and obtains the totality of person symbolized by the spherical apple. The spiritual is represented by the Virginal elements, the intellectual by the Eve-like elements, and finally the earthly desires by the Magdalene elements.

Leni, like Mary Magdalene, is regarded by the world around her as a sinner. She is constantly accosted by name callers, who refer to her as an "ausgediente Matratze" and "mieses Stuck" and "Russenliebchen." The *Verf.* emphasizes this by saying "sie hätte als Heilige (auch Magdalena) in einem Mysterienspiel auftreten können" (p. 51). Böll effectively contrasts Leni, the alleged fallen woman, and those who condemn her:[37]

> Leni Persche . . . ist es denn auch, die mit bösester Zunge über Leni spricht, sie moralisch verleumdet, obwohl sie selbst durch Vermittlung ihres Mannes, wenn überwiegend männlich Messesbesucher die Stadt überschwemmen, in einem Nachtclub sich gegen gute Bezahlung zum 'Messestrip' verdingt und . . . verkünden läßt, sie sei bereit, die Erregungen die ihre Darstellungen hervorrufen, konsequent zu befriedigen (p. 21).

---

[35]Cirlot, p. 14.

[36]*Ibid.*, p. 14.

[37]Hirsch, p. 132.

Like Katharina Mirzow, Hedwig Muller and Marie Derkum, Leni loves selflessly, first Boris and then Mehmet. Her choice of lovers is not based on externals, but on an intuitive sense of love and compassion, someone with whom she feels akin in spirit and with whom she can share her hopes. Society, which has labeled Leni sin/sex/woman/Eve, does not objectively see her actions because of her label. It has preconceived notions which make her a non-person. There is a relevant story which directly illustrates this point in the Gospel. A woman in town known as "a bad woman," ministers to Jesus, touching him, putting ointment on him and wiping his feet with her hair. Simon, Christ's host, is appalled that Jesus is not offended by her ministering acts. But Jesus perceives these as acts of devotion and ministry and love. Christian interpretation of this story has obscured *what the woman did* and concentrated on a discussion of her sinner status, or what should have been done with the expensive ointment, or what anointing meant for Jesus' coming burial. Judas the disciple, sees the use of the ointment as a waste of money and a foolish gesture. Jesus preaches at Simon, not the woman. He forgives the woman's sins without preaching. Sexual purity is not a prerequisite for ministering to Jesus. It is interesting to note that it was Jesus who was passive in receiving the ministering woman, she initiates action and He responds. Christianity has not noticed that in truth the whole story is based on the actions of an assertive, demonstrative woman.[38] Hans Schnier despises the labels, as was discussed in the prior chapter, because once a label is given to someone, his acts are no longer observed, for he/she has already been assigned a slot, a category, as Leni has by her neighbors. In this story from Luke, Jesus praises the woman extravagantly and forgives her. According to apocryphal literature, this woman is reputed to have been Mary Magdalene. It is interesting to note that although she has not asked for

---

[38]This interpretation is offered by Rachel Conrad Wahlberg, *Jesus According to Woman*, p. 52.

forgiveness, the act is often interpreted as a penitent one.

This story is recorded in all four Gospels: Matthew, Mark, John and Luke, pointing to the importance of the story. In relating a story of the two debtors to Simon, Jesus in essence tells him that this woman, whom Simon has labeled "bad," is superior to him. This is an unacceptable idea that Simon simply cannot grasp, so used is he to laying blame on the women of the street. Böll, in the characters of Leni and of Margret Schlömer, is asking modern Christians to identify with the perception of Jesus rather than that of Simon. Böll would vigorously agree with Rachel Wahlberg's criticism of misplaced interpretation of the Gospel:

> Rather than emphasize the woman's sinner label or what could have been done with her money, the interpretive emphasis should be on the activity of the woman based on her own purposeful decision to enter Simon's house with a plan in mind. Jesus' response to the woman not only leads to a verbal rebuke of Simon as judgmental and unforgiving, but indicates love, acceptance and forgiveness for the woman.[39]

Leni, Margret and the woman in this Gospel can all serve as models for women, if one is able to separate their sinner label from their acts of ministry.

Margret Schlömer, Leni's best friend of forty years, whom Böll has called the "zweite Hauptfigur des Romans"[40] is the other Mary Magdalene figure in the novel. At the opening of the novel, Margret is in the hospital suffering from an incurable venereal disease. The nurses and doctors, who brand her a prostitute, refer to her by nicknames for the male sex organs in order to tease her. Unlike Leni, Margret has an enormous

---

[39]*Ibid.*, p. 58.

[40]Wellershoff/Böll, p. 343.

feeling of shame[41] and she blushes so intensely as a result of the cruel game the employees play on her, that she dies of blushing:

> war ihr Körper mit Hämatomen und Purpur bedeckt . . . und da das Erröten bei Frau Schlömer zu einer massiven Neurose geworden war, errötete sie am Abend vor der Nacht, in dem sie starb, sogar, als die Schwestern in der Kapelle die Allerheiligenlitanei sangen (p. 391).

Much like Leni, Margret is labeled a *Freudenmädchen* and *Nutte* by society, yet she maintains a certain innocence (indicated by her death by blushing). At the age of sixteen she had discovered "es sei so wunderbar, wie die Jungen sich freuten, manche schrien vor Freude--und sie dann auch . . . (und) es machte ihr, Margret, eben Freude, ihnen Freude zu machen" (p. 49). Her generous and compassionate sensuality for others is reminiscent of Katharina Mirzow (*Im Tal der donnernden Hufe*).

Margret has had a variety of lovers in her lifetime, but she never used sex as a form of exploitation: "für Geld hatte sie sich nur verheiratet" (p. 235). Böll, in an interview, states "es war irrig, sie als Hure zu bezeichnen."[42] When she worked in the army hospital as a nurse, she gave herself freely to "jedem, der nett aussah und traurig drein blickte, voll Barmherzigkeit." She follows a code of principles in her choice of lovers. She would, however, compromise if the happiness of another was at stake. She often diverted the attention of a guard named Boldig during the times that Leni and Boris were together. She felt nothing for Boldig, but carried on with him to secure happiness for Leni and Boris.

Margret's entire life was ruled by compassion: "Sie konnte so schlecht 'Nein' sagen, wenn sie ahnte, es wäre ihr möglich, Freude zu spenden" (p. 387). Margret, "die allzu barmherzige Samaritarin" offers

---

[41]Margret is described as "ausgesprochen schamhaft" (p. 390).

[42]Wellershoff/Böll, p. 335.

Böll an opportunity to condemn a society that views her acts of compassion as prostitution and marriage as a sacrament. Margret's compassionate sensuality does not perish with her, but lives on in Leni, who is able to attract and influence others in order to allow her virtues to take root. Margret and Leni both give of themselves and their love, making their errings human and understandable, therefore forgivable. In the *Frankfurter Vorlesungen*, Böll supports his morality with reference to the New Testament:

> die Kirchen haben noch nicht begriffen, was Liebe ist, obwohl ihnen die Texte genug zur Verfügung stehen, die sie gegeneinanderstellen könnten: die großartigen Texte-
> -was übriggeblieben ist, ist eine juristische Spitzfindigkeit, um so etwas zu regeln wie Liebe und Ehe (p. 100-101).

As in *Ansichten eins Clowns*, Boll advocates here a re-evaluation of the Church and its role in society.

In the *Frankfurter Vorlesungen*, Böll addressed himself to the problem of a marriage which is loveless and "ein Liebesverhältnis, das keine Ehe ist" (p. 100). He states that from a literary standpoint, "als Material gesehen ist nichts spannender als eine feste unbeugsame Moral" (p. 101). Böll has dealt with the problem of the inflexible canon law and an individual's right to an humane interpretation of that law in a number of works, *Das Brot der frühen Jahre* (Hedwig-Walter), *Billard um halbzehn* (Edith-Robert), *Ansichten eines Clowns* (Marie-Hans).

The subject of a loveless Catholic marriage and consequent adultery is dealt with in his radio-play *Aussatz* (1969). Böll's concept of marriage, as seen in the earlier chapter, is made valid by the mutual consent of two people. Leni has participated in four "marriages," Erhard, Alois, Boris and Mehmet. She does not find love in the marriage with Alois; regarded as the only marriage legally in the eyes of the Church and state. She feels unmarried to Alois and married to the other three, an irony typical of Böll. Böll illustrates in both Leni and Margret that compassion for another person is a legitimate justification for sexual relations. This is seen dramatically in Ilse Kremer's story in *Gruppenbild mit Dame*. Mrs. Kremer and another young woman are hiding in a brewery cellar during an air raid and are justifiably frightened. Two men are hiding there with them. One of the men makes advances toward her, she finds it impossible to fight him off and describes the situation as follows:

> wir haben es eben da miteinander getrieben . . . es hört sich wohl schrecklich für Sie an, aber Sie können sich das nicht vorstellen, wenn sechseinhalb Stunden lang die Flugzeuge kommen und Bomben werfen, Luftmienen und an die sechstausend Sprengbomben--wir haben uns einfach zusammengetan, wir vier, mit dem Jüngelchen zwischen uns (p. 249).

Böll vividly illustrates that compassion is a natural human response and a compassionate sexual act is not only acceptable, but expected. In the Gospel of Luke, compassion is praised as a Christian's main social and human responsibility. Prostitutes are treated very favorably in Böll's works, for they sometimes represent the last elements of humanity in an inhuman society. This is seen in the short story, *Mein trauriges Gesicht* (1950), in which a prostitute blows a kiss to an arrested prisoner when it was required that everyone spit in his face. The prostitute is not depicted in a negative light in any of Böll's works. In *Aussatz*, a wife refers to another woman as a *Freudenmädchen*, her husband steps in to remind her what the word means -- *Mädchen der Freude* -- they bring joy and physical love, something Böll simply cannot despise.

> Ich habe die Klienten dieser (Frauen) Häuser nie verachten können, weil es mir unmöglich ist, das, was man irrigerweise die körperliche Liebe nennt, zu verachten; sie ist die Substanz eines Sakraments, und ich

zolle ihr Ehrfurcht, die ich auch dem eingeweihten Brot
als der Substanz eines Sakraments zolle.[43]

Rahel Maria Ginzburg is Leni's spiritual mother and mentor, as is
symbolized by her first name Rachel, who was the matriarch of the tribe
from which Mary and Christ descended.[44] Rahel's middle name Maria
also reinforces this unification with the Virgin Mary. Leni meets Rahel in
1939 when she attends boarding school. Rahel, a nun of Jewish origin, is
depicted as a very intelligent woman. Her academic concentration lies in
medicine, biology, and philosophy, "alles unterlegt mit einer theologischen
Beimischung, ausschließlich mystiker Herkunft" (p. 40). She bears a closer
kinship with Böhme than with modern science. During the Nazi regime,
she has been demoted to the most menial of jobs, i. e., toilet inspection of
the girls in the dormitories. Her nickname *Haruspica* refers to this side of
her personality. After Leni's expulsion and later into the war, she is kept in
the basement by the other nuns and given very little to eat. Leni is the only
one who visits and brings her food and cigarettes. Leni cannot grasp the
reason for Rahel's mistreatment by the other nuns, much as she is unable
to comprehend her fellow workers' mistreatment of Boris. Leni has no
understanding of the political implications of her simple human
compassion towards these *Untermenschen*, Boris the enemy Russian and
Rahel the Jewish nun. She simply does not comprehend "was überhaupt
ein Jude oder 'ne Jüdin ist." She is a person "der instinktiv weiß, was für
ihn richtig ist und der instinktiv immer das ihm Gemäße tut und dadurch
sich von der Gesellschaft unterscheidet und absondert, obwohl er mitten in
ihr lebt."[45]

---

[43]Heinrich Böll, *Brief an eingen jungen Katholiken* (Cologne: Kiepenheuer and
    Witsch, 1961), p. 12.

[44]Ley, p. 34.

[45]Wellershoff/Böll, p. 332.

Rahel spends the last few years of life "wie ne zum Tod verurteilte Maus" (p. 99), and perishes in a manner very similar to Margret. Rahel is labeled and categorized by the Nazi ideology as a Jew; Margret is labeled a prostitute; both are abused and mistreated by their fellow human beings, leading to their eventual death.

Upon Sister Rahel's death, roses begin to grow on her grave in the middle of winter. The *Verf.* pursues his investigation of this phenomenon by flying to Rome in order to interview another nun, Sister Klementina, who is conducting the Church's investigation into this alleged miracle. Klementina is a forty-one year old nun, who is finishing her doctoral dissertation on Gottfried Benn. Upon meeting, the *Verf.* and Klementina fall in love at first sight, an idyllic counterpart to the scene between Leni and Boris. Like Ilona, she chooses to leave the walls of the convent in order to find love. Klementina possesses both physical and intellectual charms (p. 324). She is persuaded to leave the convent after eighteen years, and leaves to follow Leni and her community and to fulfill the love she feels for the *Verf.*. Klementina's return to the world marks an important change in Böll's position. In *Nicht nur zur Weihnachtszeit*, the monastery offered a solution to ones inability to cope with a society, with whose ideals and morality one was not in agreement. Ilona retreated to the convent, but because of her deep desire for a family, she chose to leave, but becomes a war fatality. Wartime does not allow love to be fulfilled. In *Billard um halbzehn*, the abbey is presented in a very negative light, for the monks had outwardly supported the Nazis. This negative portrayal is continued in *Ansichten eines Clowns*, where the seminarians in Leo's college are in training for the priesthood. Klementina, chooses to return to the world, but equipped with intelligence, a profession and a man to share her ideals. Johanna Fähmel's return from her "innere Emigration" marked an end to withdrawal as a solution. Now, in the character of Klementina, Böll advocates an active participation by the lambs in the world.

It is interesting to note that Böll's major women characters share a love of music. Leni owns a piano, which she holds so dear "daß sie auf die Straße gehen würde, um ihr Klavier vor der Pfändung zu retten" (p. 308). In keeping with the rest of her being, she participates in music much as in religion, through an intuitive and sensual approach. A musical note, like a communion host, is merely a symbol, which has, according to Leni, very little to do with what it represents. She acts through her own grace and intuitively understands music, as well as religion and art. This natural ability is again seen when she works as a wreath maker in Pelzer's *Kranzbinderei*. She was never trained in wreath making, but is naturally talented. She is described as "Naturgenie der Garnierung" by Grundtsch, the head gardner. Leni's talent in this area is a spontaneous one.

Leni did quite well in German in school and wrote an excellent essay on Kleist's *Die Marquise von O.* Both stories, *Die Marquise von O.* and *Gruppenbild mit Dame*, are concerned with the theme of *Liebe im Krieg*. In each story, the two people involved are from enemy camps, and in both there is a "rätzelhafter Empfängnis," allowing for a virginal interpretation.[46] Both parody the Virgin birth. The Marquise von O. would rather believe "daß die Gräber befruchtet werden," than that she can be carrying a child. This theme is included in the story of Boris and Leni, for their child Lev is born in a vault in the grave yard during the war. The theme again appears in the story of Rahel. Her grave is indeed "befruchtet" in the courtyard of the cloister when roses grow in the middle of winter. A rose symbolizes completion and perfection;[47] in religious illustrations roses have always symbolized perfected love and are specifically associated with the Virgin Mary.[48]

During the course of the novel, Leni is separated from three of her

[46]Bernath, p. 53

[47]Cirlot, p. 263.

[48]Bernath, p. 53.

four lovers; first her cousin Erhard, the sensitive artist, is executed in the war and leaves her a "platonische Witwe;" Alois Pfeiffer, the *Verführer*, is killed three days after their marriage, which the *Verf.* dubs an "existentiellen Fehltritt;" Boris, the Soviet "subhuman" with whom she shared a *Sowjetparadies* and from whom she bears a child, is killed in a French labor camp. For Mehmet, the Muslim *Gastarbeiter*, to whom she shows compassion and from whom she is expecting a child, the future does not appear to be secure either. At the close of the novel, it is hinted that "Gewitterwolken" were becoming visible in the background. Mehmet's jealousy and repugnance for social dancing promises to be a source of conflict.

But Leni survives the war, the loss of her family, the death of her closest friends (Rahel, Margret), the loss of her lovers (Erhard, Boris), the material ethos of the restoration with her *Mitmenschlichkeit* totally intact. Thus in this novel we have seen a woman move for the first time from the periphery of the action to occupy a role of central importance. Leni acts and thinks independently, and influences all those around her. Moreover, in a period of great instability, she survives not as others have, by being shrewd and calculating, but by emphasizing these maternal and loving features Böll's positive women have always displayed. In the next chapter we will see how in *Katharina Blum* Böll's woman becomes not only central, but active as a protagonist.

Chapter Four

"Die heilige Katharina"

Die verlorene Ehre der Katharina Blum concerns itself with the murder trial of Katharina Blum. Böll in his own words best summarizes the plot:

> am Mittwoch, dem 20. 2. 1974, am Vorabend von Weiberfastnacht, verläßt in einer Stadt eine junge Frau von siebenundzwanzig Jahren abends gegen 18.45 ihre Wohnung, um an einem privaten Tanzvergnügen teilzunehmen.
>
> Vier Tage später, nach einer . . . dramatischen Entwicklung, am Sonntagabend um fast die gleiche Zeit-- genauer gesagt gegen 19.04--, klingelt sie an der Wohnungstür des Kriminaloberkommissars Walter Moeding, der eben dabei ist, sich aus dienstlichen, nicht privaten gründen als Scheich zu verkleiden, und gibt dem erschrockenen Moeding zu Protokoll, sie habe mittags gegen 12.15 in ihrer Wohnung den Journalisten Werner Tötges erschossen, er möge veranlassen daß ihre Wohnungstür aufgebrochen und er dort 'abgeholt' werde; sie selbst habe sich zwischen 12.15 und 19.00 Uhr in der Stadt herumgetrieben, um Reue zu finden, habe aber keine Reue gefunden; sie bitte ausserdem um ihre Verhaftung, sie möchte gern dort sein, wo auch ihr 'lieber Ludwig,' sei.[1]

The story of Katharina Blum's life and character unfolds as a number of people give testimony about her. Once more Böll has chosen the documentary format for his work, and as in *Ende einer Dienstfahrt*, the action revolves around a legal trial. Our informants are called upon to

---

[1]Heinrich Böll, *Die verlorene Ehre der Katharina Blum* (Cologne: Kiepenheuer & Witsch, 1974), p. 9.

testify as to Katharina Blum's character.

The question that becomes paramount in the mind of the reader is what would move such a responsible young woman as Katharina to murder. This theme is stated in the subtitle itself: *Wie Gewalt entstehen und wohin sie führen kann.*

Katharina Blum is the household manager for Hubert and Trude Blorna. Hubert Blorna is a corporation attorney and his wife, Trude is an architect. Katharina is an outstanding housekeeper as attested to by Hubert Blorna:

> Wie wir Katharina zu Dank verpflichtet sind: seit sie ruhig und freundlich, auch planvoll unseren Haushalt leitet, sind nicht nur unsere Unkosten erheblich gesunken, sie hat uns auch beide für unsere berufliche Arbeit so frei gemacht, daß wir es kaum in Geld ausdrücken können. Sie hat uns von dem fünfjährigen Chaos befreit, das unsere Ehe und unsere berufliche Arbeit so belastet hat (pp. 39-40).

Katharina's father was a miner before his death when Katharina was six years old. Her mother worked as a cleaning woman to support the family. With the help of her godmother, Else Woltersheim, Katharina was able to go to school to become a housekeeper. She completed her studies with an outstanding academic record. In 1968 she married a textile worker, Wilhelm Brettloh, whom she left a few months later, "weil er immer häufiger zudringlich wurde." She obtained a divorce and took back her maiden name. She accepted a position with Dr. Fehnern, a certified public accountant, as a housekeeper and attended evening classes in order to complete her "Fachprüfung als staatlich geprüfte Wirtschafterin." She then found a position with the Blornas, for whom she has worked for the past four years.

Katharina is invited to a party hosted by Else Woltersheim. She is very excited to go because she enjoys dancing very much. Her scruples normally restrict her dancing activities:

> da gab es, wie sie Blornas erzählte diese Buden, in denen
> eigentlich nur verklemmte Studenten eine kostenlose
> Nutte suchen, dann gab es diese bohemenartigen Dinger,
> in denen es ihr ebenfalls zu wüst zuging, und
> konfessionelle Tanzveranstaltungen verabscheute sie
> geradezu (p. 54).

By coincidence Ludwig Götten appears at the same party. When the "als prüde bekannte" Katharina dances with him, the two are immediately infatuated with one another, "fast und sofort mit Beschlag." They are described as dancing "ausschließlich und innig . . . als würden sie sich schon ewig kennen" (p. 71).[2]

Ludwig Götten is being sought by the police for desertion from the *Bundeswehr* and possible involvement in a murder and robbery case. Once more Böll depicts a love story under the most adverse conditions. Götten, it turns out later, is not guilty of any crime except desertion. Katharina shows him a route of escape from the police. In a dramatic sequel she is brought in for questioning and is suspected of aiding his escape. The story makes the headline of the *Bild Zeitung* -- "Räuberliebchen Katharina Blum verweigert Aussage über Herrenbesuche." A journalist named Werner Tötges covers the story, emphasizing especially the sexual overtones of the story, as is typical of a sensational paper such as *Bild*. As a result of his articles, she is accosted with letters, cards and telephone calls offering sexual services and cursing her. Katharina loses her respect and position in society (*Rufmord*) through these articles. The journalist goes so far as to

---

[2] Böll uses the dance as a symbol in much the same vein as he employed *Handauflegung* in *Gruppenbild mit Dame*. Linked dances generally symbolizes "a cosmic matrimony, or the union of heaven and earth -- the chain symbol -- in this way they facilitate the union of man and wife." It is interesting to note that Böll has chosen a cosmic matrimony (dance) in *Katharina Blum* and a mystical matrimony (*Handauflegung*) in *Gruppenbild mit Dame*. (Cirlot, p. 73).

sneak into the hospital room of Katharina's mother for an interview. Katharina's mother is in the intensive care unit recovering from extensive cancer surgery. Her statements to the journalist are distorted in his article. Rather than stating "mußte es so kommen, mußte es so enden," he rewrites it as "ich wußte es würde so kommen, so mußte es ja enden." He defends this change in the statement, "daß er als Reporter drauf eingestellt und gewohnt sei, 'einfachen Menschen Artikulationshilfe zu geben'" (p. 107). Katharina's mother dies as a result of the shock of the news told to her by Tötges.

Katharina's childhood had changed dramatically as a result of a similar sensational distortion. Her mother was caught in the sacristy with the verger, sharing a bottle of sacramental wine. This incident became grossly exaggerated and soon was amplified as "the orgy that occured in the sacristy." Prior to this incident Katharina is described as "fromm und kirchentreu" (p. 66). Thereafter Katharina was mistreated by the priest, resulting perhaps in her being teased by her playmates and teachers in school. Katharina would blush with embarrassment when the priest would refer to her as "unser rötliches Kathrinchen" (p. 142). The whole class would laugh, "ich wußte gar nicht was er meinte, und die ganze Klasse lachte, weil ich dann rot wurde" (p. 142).

At the age of nineteen she left the Catholic Church, although she would still go to church "nicht aus religiösen Gründen, sondern weil man da Ruhe hat, aber auch in Kirchen werden Sie neuerdings angequatscht, und nicht nur von Laien" (p. 50). Her religion is an interior one. When asked to say a prayer for her recently deceased mother, Katharina shakes her head and says *Nein*, and places a loving kiss on her forehead instead. Through this kiss, Katharina expresses clearly her compassion for her mother and her fellow human beings. She can no longer find solace or consolation in a prayer.

The similarities between Katharina Blum and Leni Pfeiffer are striking. In speaking of his novel, *Gruppenbild mit Dame*, Böll characterized it as being basically "nur eine Liebesgeschichte...eine Liebe...in eine möglichst schwierige, heikle, politisch, sozial...schwierige Situation."[3] This statement describes the situation in his latest work as well. In the case of Katharina, we are not in a war setting, but in the equally oppressive restorative society. Böll chooses a criminal named Ludwig Götten to be the equally undesirable equivalent to Boris, both are regarded as *Untermenschen* by society and ostracised by them. The journalist refers to Ludwig as an *Unmensch*: "Soll man gegen Unmenschen menschlich bleiben müssen" (p. 118). The irony is unmistakeable in light of Götten's innocence and Tötges' guilt.

Upon meeting their lovers, the lives of both Katharina and Leni change radically. Upon first meeting Ludwig, Katharina tells her friends: "Ich fühlte Zärtlichkeit für ihn und er für mich" (p. 36). Katharina is vehement about distinguishing the words *Zudringlichkeit* and *Zärtlichkeit* during the trial. The word *zudringlich* is used in her descriptions of men, by whom she is repulsed: her husband Wilhelm Brettloh--"(sie habe) sich von ihrem Mann scheiden lassen, weil er *zudringlich* geworden ist;" Dr. Kluthen by whom she was employed until "Herr Doktor immer häufiger *zudringlich* wurde" (p. 23); and the men she met at the Blornas' social gatherings, "es kam, da die Herren oft angetrunken waren, auch dort zu *Zudringlichkeit*" (p. 29). She defines *Zärtlichkeit* as "eine beiderseitige" and *Zudringlichkeit* as "eine einseitige Handlung" (p. 30).

Physically both Leni and Katharina are very attractive and no man seems to be able to resist them, reminding us of Eve, a temptation to all

---

[3] Böll/Wellershoff, p. 337. "While this statement may at first seem surprising from a man whose reputation rests in large measure on the powerful presentation in his work of pacifistic, and socialistic values and his unrelenting treatment of Germany's war guilt, the fact remains that whether Böll's work treats the madness of the Hitler years of the greed and complacency of the 'economic miracle,' central to his stories is usually a love relationship." *Ibid.*, p. 36.

who gaze upon her. Both spend considerable time fighting off "immer häufiger zudringliche Männer, which neither of them resist "aus moralischen, sondern aus Geschmacksgründen" (*Katharina Blum*, p. 112).

Böll's choice of names for Katharina Blum is as deliberate as his choice of Helena Maria Pfeiffer, both names lend considerable insight into the bearers' personality and nature. Böll's development of the woman figure is a gradual one and finds its culmination in Katharina Blum. Whereas Leni Pfeiffer was depicted as a model of private virtue, Katharina Blum is not only a model, but is depicted as a saint.

This thesis is supported by the documentary format that Böll has chosen for his latest two works. It has been suggested that the *Verf.* in *Gruppenbild mit Dame* can be viewed as the promoter of the cause,[4] or solicitor, who has been appointed by the Church to gather information regarding the character of persons in question, their reputation for holiness and the miracles that have been performed by them.[5] This would be in keeping with the *Verf.*'s statement that he is undertaking this "unermüdliche Rechierarbeit," "im Dienst der Wahrheit." The documentary format would allow Böll to ingeniously link "ein uraltes kirchliches Ritual mit dem gegenwärtig sehr beliebten literarischen Dokument."[6] Ziolkowski views this as an innovation "in der Anwendung einer säkularisierten kirchlichen Form, *um das Thema einer säkukalisierten christlichen Heiligkeit* adäquat zu gestalten."[7]

Böll discussed a desire to reawaken the spirits of the canonized saints of the Church in an interview with Karin Struck. He expressed a concern

---

[4]Ziolkowski, "Typologie un 'Einfache Form.'" p. 138.

[5]*Encyclopedia International* (New York: Grolier, Inc., 1963) p. 136.

[6]Ziolkowski, p. 136.

[7]Ziolkowski, p. 138.

that the saints had become "rein, fixiert, im Grunde getötet."[8] They had become static pictures on the wall and statues on desks, not live models to whom modern man could relate. He viewed his task as an artist "den Heiligen von der Wand und Wieder-zum-Leben-Bringen."[9] It is the contention of this study that he does precisely this in Katharina Blum. He removes the plastic image of St. Catherine of Siena, the first political saint of the Church, from the wall and gives her a modern setting in which to live. The basic question is the same as in *Gruppenbild mit Dame*. Can such innocence and purity exist in a contemporary society? In *Gruppenbild mit Dame*, Böll acknowledged that question with a strong affirmative, so much so that he offered an alternative non-profit society (Müllkutscher) as a solution to a materialistic and shallow society.

Canonization Process

An analysis of Böll's documentary format in *Gruppenbild mit Dame* and *Katharina Blum* lends proof to Böll's contention that his work must be viewed as a *Fortschreibung*. The canonization process consists of three basic steps, all of which are in evidence in all of Böll's works to some degree, culminating in the final step, canonization of sainthood-- Katharina Blum. Böll finally canonizes his woman figure, a model for all to follow.

Böll's early works depict woman as a nursing, loving and forgiving creature, able to heal man through her love and compassion. He is the central figure and she is the passive good woman supporting him. The woman is an *Engelfigur*, who alone is able to offer consolation and hope to man in the meaningless existence of war. The virtues of womanhood are praised by Böll in these works and her nature is firmly established in the mind of the readers.

---

[8]Karin Struck/Heinrich Böll, "Schreiben un Lesen," in *Einmischung Erwünscht* (Cologne: Kiepenheuer and Witsch, 1977), p. 64.

[9]*Ibid.*, p. 63.

The next phase of Böll's woman views her as an individual willing to voice her protest against the persecution by the *Büffel* (Johanna Fähmel). As an individual act, this protest is bound to have little success and effect, but nevertheless it is an active protest. In *Gruppenbild mit Dame* the private and offensive protest gains support by a group of believers or adherents, who follow Leni Pfeiffer's lead in establishing an alternative society. Enough support is gained that a *Verf.*, or solicitor, is sent out to gather all the information possible with regards to the character of the person, her reputation and possible miracles that she may have worked. The solicitor's job is to elicit statements from as many persons as possible to promote her cause. In the canonization process his report would be forwarded to the tribunal of the Congregation of Rites. If the tribunal passes favorable judgment, the person is elevated to the rank of "venerable servant" and step two is set in motion. More intensive investigation is made (*Katharina Blum*). Besides the solicitor, a "Devil's Advocate" is added, whose task is to find weaknesses in the case presented. This role is accorded to the reader himself in *Gruppenbild mit Dame* and *Katharina Blum*. It is his/her job to view the situation critically, and come to a proper conclusion, a clever and unique way to involve the reader. If the objections of the "Devil's Advocate" are answered, the candidate is raised to the ranks of the *Blessed*, a ceremony known as beatification. *Gruppenbild mit Dame* ends on this step. The final step involves deeper investigation into the miracles worked since the beatification, and if they are proven genuine, she is raised to the rank of Saint and all must venerate her in the Church.[10]

Catherine of Siena

Katharina comes from the Greek word Katharos, (Κατηαροσ), meaning "pure one." Her last name Blum could be symbolic of beauty, but in conjunction with Katharina would appear to be a reference to Catherine

---

[10]*Encyclopedia International*, p. 67.

of Siena, whose symbol is a lily.[11] Both come from a background of little learning, social standing or wealth. At the age of seven, Katharina's life changed drastically when her mother is caught drinking wine in the sacristy. From that day on she is referred to as "unser rötliches Kathrinchen." At the same age Catherine vowed her virginity to Christ, following a vision of Christ. Catherine received the stigmata at the age of twenty-eight, the same age Katharina has her encounter with Götten:

> *Mein Gott*, er war es eben, der da kommen soll, und ich hätte ihn geheiratet und Kinder mit ihm gehabt--und wenn ich hätte warten müssen jahrelang (Emphasis added, p. 61).

The lives of both women are filled with great pain and adversity, which they not only overcome, but bear with nobility.

The best known episode about Catherine ocurred in 1377 with her meeting with Niccolo de Tuldo, a young man sentenced to death on a charge of sedition. He had uttered some rash words against the government. By the same token, the central event of Katharina's life occurs with her encounter with Ludwig Götten, alleged murderer, robber and deserter. It is interesting to note that when Götten is finally brought to trial, he is found guilty of desertion alone, also a form of political protest against the government.

Niccolo had been described as hard and bitter, refusing to make his confession and raging with despair. Catherine was summoned to bring him some comfort. When Catherine drew his head to her breast, he became "like a meek lamb led to the sacrifice.[12] He asked her to come to the place

---

[11]The color symbols can of course be viewed from a political standpoint, alluding to Böll's liberal left leanings and recent support of Leftist causes, but since "politics is on the periphery of his mahor works...at the center is the relationship of a man and a woman." Conrad, p. 36.

[12]Edmund G. Gardner, *Saint Catherine of Siena* (London: T.M. Dent & Co., 1907), p. 211.

of execution and when she promised that she would, he said, "I shall go wholly joyous and strong and it will be to me a thousand years before I arrive, since you are awaiting me there."[13] He died with Christ's name and Catherine's name on his lips and she received his severed head into her hands. She had encountered this young man by chance, much as Katharina encounters Ludwig. She was able to save his rebellious soul, "it was her capacity for compassionate tenderness that explains her power over people."[14] These words could very well have been written about Leni and Katharina. Both Catherines show a spirit of self-sacrificing devotion to others. Katharina Blum, for instance, helps an older couple, the Hiepertz, on a regular basis: "nicht ums Geld, nein, für solche Gefälligkeiten dürfen wir ihr gar nichts anbieten, das würde sie tief kränken" (*Katharina Blum*, p. 16).

As was previously noted, Katharina had left the Church at the age of nineteen and is very critical of both Church and the clergy. Böll, in his depiction of priests, once again denounces them fiercely. Catherine of Siena was also a vehement critic of the clergy of her time. A sampling of her criticism follows:

> They have chosen for their table the public tavern, and there, openly cursing and perjuring themselves, full of many miserable sins, like men blinded and without the light of reason, have become animals through their sins, and live lasciviously in word and deed . . .[15]

Catherine wanted the Church to "return to her first condition, poor, humble and meek, as she was in that holy time when men took note of nothing but the honour of God and the salvation of souls, caring for

---

[13]Theodore Maynard, *Saints of Our Times* (New York: Image Books, 1952), p. 74.

[14]*Ibid.*, p. 74.

[15]*Ibid.*, p. 76.

spiritual things not for temporal.[16]

Catherine was persecuted by her family for not wanting to marry and was compelled to do all the drudgery work at home. Katharina married to escape the "schreckliche(n) häusliche(n) Milieu" (p. 66). Catherine carried out the work joyfully, feeling compelled to suffer as much as possible in order to come closer to God. She took the habit of the Sisters of Penance of St. Dominic, called the "Mantellate" in Siena wearing the white robe of innocence and the black mantle of humility. They were not nuns, but devoted themselves to the service of God in their own homes. After accepting the habit, Catherine kept complete silence for three years, speaking only with her confessor Fra Tommaso della Fonte. During this period she began having visions, in which the Lord communicated with her. She became the 'mystical bride of Christ' at this time as well.[17]

During her free time, Catherine would weave flower crosses and garlands singing mystical songs the while,[18] a likely source for Leni Pfeiffer's wartime job. She returned to life with her family in 1366 to heal and to convert souls.[19] Leni also was attributed with having cured her little boy by applying saliva to his wound. As with Leni and Katharina,

---

[16]John Ferguson, *An Illustrated Encyclopedia of Mysticism & the Mystery of Religions* (New York: Seabury Press, 1977), p. 37.

[17]Catherine's espousal occurred when she was twenty, on Shrove Tuesday 1367. The Lord appeared to her and revealed that He had determined to celebrate the feast of espousal to Him. He placed Himself as her side, along with the Virgin Mary and the apostles St. John and St. Paul served as witnesses. He placed a ring upon her finger, set with a diamond circled by four pearls. He pronounced the following ritual: "I, your Creator and your Savior, wed you in this vow which until you celebrate with Me in Heaven our eternal nuptials, will preserve you spotless...armed with the power of faith you will successfully oversome all your adversitities: Ignio Giordani, *Saint Catherine of Siena*, trans. Thomas J. Tobin (Bosti: Paulist Press, 1959), p. 44. This mystical espousal reminds us of the *Heidekrauterlebnis* Leni experienced.

[18]Gardner, p. 22.

[19]*Ibid.*, p. 47.

persecution followed Catherine of Siena throughout her public ministries. Especially the women distrusted her conduct and her mode of life[20] "her sisters in religion reviled and slandered her, and called upon their superiors to correct her. They even gained over some of the Dominican friars to their side, who refused to have any dealing with her and often *deprived her of the Blessed Sacrament in Communion*, and even for a while took away her faithful confessor from her"[21] (Emphasis added). Like Leni, she took communion every day, "it was not only the center of her whole inner life, but her very bodily existence depended on it."[22] Leni, despite abuse by her neighbors, goes to the bakery daily for her fresh *Brötchen*, "worauf sie den größten Wert legt" (p. 11).

In describing Catherine, Fra Bartolommeo stated "her aspect and address seemed to pour forth a certain fragrance of purity, more angelical than human, and withal she was always joyful and merry of countenance."[23] This could very well be a description of Leni, given by one of the informants. The *Verf.*, in an attempt to define Leni, looks up the word *Unschuld* in the dictionary, because that concept must be fully understood to comprehend Leni. She radiates "rein naive Mitmenschlichkeit" (p. 139) and her disposition "doch ein wahrer Sonnenschein, wenn die Leni mal was sang . . . man konnte schon sehen, hören und auch spüren, daß sie nicht nur verliebt war, auch geliebt wurde" (p. 220). Catherine also loved to sing, "her voice, though rather thin was sweet, and she put her soul into it."[24]

Blorna describes Katharina's nature and his "Ehrfurcht vor ihrer, ja

---

[20]*Ibid.*, p. 50.

[21]*Ibid.*, p. 50.

[22]*Ibid.*, p. 52.

[23]*Ibid.*, p. 53.

[24]Giordani, p. 121.

verdammt, Unschuld--und mehr, mehr als Unschuld" (p. 90). All of these women are described as possessing and radiating innocence, which is a large part of their nature.

Catherine is characterized as having "extraordinary charm and almost masculine strength of mind."[25] This statement could well be made by one of the witnesses about Katharine Blum. Unlike Böll's previous women figures, she possesses something of the "masculine strength of mind." Katharina's hands become masculine *Schießhände* and *Scheckschreibendehände*, yet she still is very much a charming, innocent and beautiful woman.

Catherine attracted numerous followers who left their families to follow her. Her followers were called *caterinati*, children of Catherine, but Catherine herself called them "our group."[26] Many served her as secretaries "binding themselves to her in worship and love of friendship; a spiritual tie of whole-hearted devotion."[27] Many approached her with the intention of saying everything bad about her, but in her presence they could not utter a word: "Haughty youths, wealthy patricians whom she won over to God turned their backs upon comforts and frivolities to follow her and be enrolled in the magic circle of her love."[28] Her whole family of followers "rested upon her, lived in her. Each of them, one by one, encountered crises in their lives and all of them one by one were raised from earth to heaven by those *transparent hands* which divine love had pierced."[29] Leni possesses the same type of magnetism, attracting and converting them (*Gruppe*) to her humanitarian ways, teaching them

---

[25]*Colliers Encyclopedia* (New York: P.F. Collier, Inc., 1977), p. 561.

[26]Giordani, p. 117.

[27]Gardner, p. 85.

[28]Giordani, p. 119.

[29]*Ibid.*, pp. 122-123

Mitmenschlichkeit.

Catherine's spiritual and mystical writings rank among the classics of Italy.[30] The philosophy that underlies all of her writings is the same-- "love is the one and supreme and all important, all embracing, all enduring, limitless and boundless thing."[31] a theme that underlies all of Böll's novels by his own admission: "im Grunde interessieren mich als Autor nur zwei Themen: die Liebe und die Religion."[32]

It is interesting to note that the development of Böll's female figures can be traced by analyzing the three females he has given the surname of Katharina: Käte Bogner is depicted as a totally passive, religious and patient woman, who accepts her fate without saying "a mumbalin' word." Katharina Mirzow reaches out to Paul and is able to divert him from turning his gun on himself. Katharina Blum controls her own life and will defend herself forcefully if necessary to preserve her self-respect and individuality. Not only does she aim and fire her gun in protest, but she kills, survives and returns to her state of innocence.

The similarities between Leni and Katharina are numerous, but there are also some noticeable differences. Leni is characterized as being totally devoid of a profit motive and naive in business matters. This does not hold true for Katharina. She has worked hard to finish her schools and has acquired a nice apartment and car. To make a little extra income she works for a catering service on the side. She handles her finances capably. She is a very competent manager, Blorna claims they have cut down their household expenses immensely since they employed her. While she is serving her prison sentence for murdering Tötges, she thinks about the interest her money will have accumulated by the time of her release at

---

[30]Gardner, p. 353.

[31]*Ibid.*, p. 377.

[32]"Interview von Reich-Ranicki," p. 510.

thirty five years of age. She is a model prisoner in jail ("vorbildliche Gefangene," p. 131) and

> wird in die Wirtschaftsabteilung (Ökonomie) versetzt werden...dort...erwartet man sie keineswegs begeistert: man fürchtet auf Verwaltungs-und auf Häftlingsseite-- den Ruf der Korrektheit, mit planischer Intelligenz verbunden, ist nirgendwo erwünscht, nicht einmal in Gefängnissen, und nicht einmal von der Verwaltung (p. 131).

Leni, on the other hand, was described a being gifted in the areas of writing and art, but abstract concepts such as math were difficult for her.

Eva-Maria-Magdalena

It was discovered in the previous chapter that Leni fulfilled the characteristics of Böll's ideal woman as prophesied in his *Frankfurter Vorlesungen*. She was a combination of three women, "Eva, Maria, Magdalena, die sich nie rein, nie getrennt zeigen in der weiblichen Natur."[33] This *Trinität des Weiblichen* is also seen in *Katharina Blum*.

Katharina is physically very attractive and desired by many men. When she stays to help with the parties hosted by the Blornas, she dances with the men, all of whom find her "äußerst attraktive" (p. 20). Alois Sträubleder is a very wealthy industrialist, who has futilely pursued Katharina for months, presenting her with gifts. "Er habe Blumen geschickt, Briefe geschrieben, und es sei ihm einige Male gelungen, zu ihr in die Wohnung vorzudringen, bei dieser Gelegenheit habe er ihr den Ring einfach zugedrängt." He is the man the neighbors see visiting Katharina, and whose visits are dubbed *Herrenbesuche* by them and the newspaper, causing her moral reputation to be ruined. She refuses to name him to the police because she feels no one would believe that nothing had happened between them:

---

[33]Heinrich Böll, *Frankfurter Vorlesungen*, p. 100.

> Wer würde ihr schon glauben, daß sie einem Menschen
> wie Sträubleder widerstehen würde, der ja nicht nur
> wohlhabend sei, sondern in Politik Wirtschaft und
> Wissenschaft eines unwiderstehlichen Charmes wegen
> geradezu gerühmt sei, fast wie ein Filmschauspieler, und
> wer würde einer Hausangestellten wie ihr schon
> glauben, daß sie einem Filmschauspieler widerstehen
> würde (p. 112).

The other reason for her silence is that she passed on a key to Sträubelder's vacation villa to Ludwig as a hiding place. Had she told the police, they would have known where to arrest him.

Like Magdalene, Katharina is unjustly denounced by those around her. Those who really know her attest to her innocence and high standards. She is accosted with floods of cards and telephone calls:

> sieben anonyme Postkarten, handschriftlich mit 'derben
> sexuellen Offerten, die alle irgendwie das Wort
> 'Kommunistensau' verwendet hatten . . . zwei Briefe
> enthielten religiöse Ermahnungen, in beiden Fällen auf
> beigelegte Traktate geschrieben, "Du mußt wieder beten
> lernen, armes, verlorenes Kind" und "knie wieder und
> bekenne, Gott hat dich noch nicht aufgegeben" (p. 80).

The innocent and pure side of Katharina's nature is inherent in her name alone, much as it was with Leni. Her friends and relatives have given her the nickname "Nonne" (p. 54). Her employer and friend Hubert Blorna who has defined Katharina with the words "verdammte Unschuld," is totally committed to Katharina and to proving her innocence.

Only Dr. Blorna, because of a feeling of "Ehrfurcht vor ihrer . . . Unschuld," does not approach Katharina about his feeling for her. Dr. Blorna is demoted in his position with the corporation to performing menial tasks, "eine Degradierung" (pp. 125-130). He undergoes a complete change, "eine erhebliche Veränderung;" his clothes are "vernachläßigt," and "er betreibe nicht mehr ein Minimum an Körperpflege und beginne zu riechen." Utmost in his mind is still Katharina, "Kein Zweifel: er liebt sie, sie ihn nicht, und er hat nicht die geringste Hoffnung, denn alles, alles gehört doch ihrem 'lieben Ludwig.'"

The *Händchenhalten* symbol is again used by Böll, in this case between Katharina and Blorna. This holding of hands is one-sided, "denn es besteht lediglich darin, daß er, wenn Katharina Akten oder Notizen oder Aktennotizen hinüberreicht, seine Hände auf ihre legt, länger, vielleicht drei, vier, höchstens fünf zehntel Sekundel länger als üblich wäre" (p. 137).An attempt has been made as well to fire Trude Blorna from her position with an architectural firm "wegen des Vertrauensbruches." She had revealed the foundation plans of the apartment complex to Katharina. The first attempt to have her fired does not succeed "aber niemand ist sicher, wie die zweite und die dritte Instanz entscheiden werden" (p. 127). They have already had to sell their second car and the newspaper recently carried a picture of them getting into their *Superschlitten* with the caption: "Wann wird der rote Anwalt auf den Wagen des kleinen Mannes umsteigen müßen" (p. 127).

Leni was able to survive the tragedies and personal losses of forty-four years "fast unverletzt" and still remains an innocent and pure individual. Katharina is twenty-seven when she kills Tötges, an act which changed her life radically within a four day period. Like Leni, she survives and feels neither *Reue* nor *Bedauern* about her actions. She survives "fast unverletzt," as evidenced by the plans she is making for the future while in jail.

Prior to Katharina, women who were characterized or depicted as "selbstbewußt insofern als sie Geld zu schätzen wußten,"[34] like Ulla Wickweber (*Das Brot der frühen Jahre*) and Bertha (*Wie in schlechten*

[34]Schwarz, p. 82.

Romanen), were depicted in a negative light. Leni Pfeiffer of course places no value on money, all she understood was to share it with those she loved. Katharina acquires the necessities for a "good life" by working overtime to afford them. She saved 7,000 DM in a two year period to put a down-payment on her condominium. She is described as being *klug, kühl, intelligent,* and *planend.* In prison she is quickly promoted to the *Wirtschaftsabteilung.* Her reputation of "Korrektheit mit planischer Intelligenz" (p. 131) has already been widely spread.

Johanna Fähmel had voiced her protest against an oppressive society by shooting a government employee, a representative or symbol of those responsible for this oppression. Her shot wounds, but Katharina's shot finds its mark and kills. Johanna's act is explained away by her "insanity," but Katharina's action cannot be so lightly dismissed.

Katharina agreed to meet with Tötges, in order to see what kind of man it was who would employ his newspaper articles as a weapon to shatter her reputation and very existence in the community. Upon meeting her, he suggests a sexual prelude to the interview, reducing the sexual act verbally to "bumsen." She replies "bumsen, meinetwegen" and shoots him: "er wollte doch bumsen, und ich habe gebumst, oder?" (p. 142). Katharina succeeds in doing away with the perpetrator of evil. Katharina is portrayed as duly justified in destroying such an evil creature, in that she is acting in accord with her own existential perspective of morality: "er wäre der Kerl, der mich nachts angerufen hat und der auch die arme Else dauernd belästigt hat...ich wollte ihn noch ein bißchen quatschen lassen, um es herauszukriegen, aber was hätte mir das genutzt?" (p. 142).

After having committed the murder of the journalist, she enters the church next door and thinks for half an hour about her mother's life and "dieses verfluchte elende Leben, das sie gehabt hat" (p. 142). She seems to return to the traditional retreat, viewed here as a sanctuary, where she is temporarily free from society's wrath. This appears to be a return to the traditional values, to some type of moral code: "dann bin ich aus der Kirche raus und ins nächst beste Kino, und wieder raus aus dem Kino, und wieder in eine Kirche, weil das an einem Karnevalssonntag der einzige Ort war, wo man ein bißchen Ruhe fand" (p. 142). Only here can she quietly and consciously reflect upon life as a whole. She sees no need to repent for her actions, as she does not regard them as sins.

The return to the traditional is also to be noted in Böll's female figures in general. The women all reveal the characteristics considered traditional female qualities. They all are loving, compassionate and innocent. They minister to their men's needs and sacrifice their all for them. Their own reputation and respect are irreparably damaged by their contact with these men and they come to be regarded as "Abfall" by society. The women are allowed professions, the most positively drawn women all seem to achieve success in academic areas.[35]

This is best seen in the example of Klementina, who has achieved success in the area of *Germanistik*. Upon meeting the *Verf.*, she leaves the convent to follow him[36] and to join Leni's circle of friends. *Klementina* is reincarnated as *Katharina*. Katharina is very much in control of her life. Like Klementina, she is characterized as *klug, intelligent* and *kühl*. She seems like a strong willed and efficient person. Yet when she encounters a man for whom she feels *Zärtlichkeit*, she freely chooses to surrender to him, not at all in keeping with what would be expected of her. Katharina is able, like Leni before her, to overcome and ignore her environment and to follow "some internal infallible compass of her own."[37]

---

[35]Olina is an accomplished pianist; Ilona has completed her *Staatsexamen* in *Germanistik* and music; Hedwig was attending teacher's college; Rahel is a physician and researcher; Klementina is getting her doctorate in *Germanistik*.

[36]She leaves a secure future to follow a man who cannot offer her security, as he, like Hans Schnier, is practicing a "brotlose Kunst."

[37]Deschner, p. 12.

108

Whereas Leni is totally indifferent to property and profit, Katharina desires a few comforts of life; a good job, a nice apartment, and social intercourse. She does not achieve these through shrewdness or exploitation, but through honest hard work, done with her hands. It is interesting to note that all of Böll's positive male figures from Andreas to Boris and the *Verf.* worked at jobs that required the use of their hands. Never are they businessmen, clergymen, or industrialists. Katharina's hands are not only loving and caring female hands, but are capable of becoming "Schießhände" and "Scheckschreibendehände," qualities Böll had previously exclusively reserved for his negative male figures. But Böll reconciles these apparently irreconcilable values in Katharina Blum. She is described as "klug", "planend," "fleißig," and "ordentlich,"; yet "hilfsbereit," "zärtlich," "fromm" and "unschuldig." Her female nature is good and virtuous, but she is no longer depicted as the "Holy Fool," in the sense of *das Mädchen* or Käte Bogner. Katharina is prepared to lead the attack against the oppressive *Büffel*, even if this requires an act of violence.

The attack on the *Büffel* was prefigured by Johanna Fühmel, but her individual act could be dismissed as an aberration. Katharina cannot be dismissed as an "unglückliche Sonderling, und verzweifelte Außenseiter." She does not fit the category of eccentrics Böll formerly depicted. Katharina is a self-actualized woman, able to fulfill her physical needs (hunger, thirst, sex), her security needs (shelter protection) and her social needs (affection, love).[38] She directs her own life and despite the numerous adversities she encounters, survives with her self-esteem intact.

Böll's shift in his latest two works to focus on the sensual and compassionate woman figure marks a significant literary break as well. When the male dominated his action, the anger and hostility toward the status quo was Böll's major concern. With the appearance of *Gruppenbild*

---

[38]Abraham Maslow, *Toward a Psychology of Being* (Princeton: VanNostrand, 1962).

mit Dame and *Katharina Blum,* Böll suggests an alternative solution to withdrawal and isolation. His focus is on a woman figure of virtue, who shines in an evil world and illuminates the vice around her. Woman attests to the fact that private virtue can endure the worst afflictions and survive with innocence intact.

Chapter Five

The Woman As Survivor

The position of woman is often considered a test by which the level of civilization of a country may be judged. In the *Frankfurter Vorlesungen*, Böll lamented the role to which woman had been relegated in much of modern literature--to what he dubs a *Lustspieleva* and *Lustspielmagdalena*. In his depiction of the *Trinität des Weiblichen* (Eva, Maria and Magdalena), prophesied in the *Frankfurter Vorlesungen*, Böll has attempted to create or recreate the three-fold nature of his ideal woman, stressing the very important and seemingly neglected virginal side to the female.

Böll's religion is solidly grounded in Catholicism. He attended a Catholic grade school and then the *Gymnasium*, receiving the *Abitur* in 1937. Although Böll has offered massive criticism against the Catholic Church as an institution and the clergy in particular, he has not left the Church, because, as he states: "Ich brauche die Sakramente, ich brauche die Liturgie, aber ich brauche den Klerus nicht -- grob besagt -- als Institution."[1] In an interview with Karin Struck, Böll discussed his Catholic upbringing "in einer ikonischen Welt . . . wo die Heiligen . . . auch die Madonna rein waren."[2] Böll felt great admiration for many of the canonized saints of the Church, but felt that through canonization these models of virtue had become somehow "rein, fixiert, im Grunde getötet."[3] It was almost impossible to relate to them because they appeared as such irreproachable static "pictures." As an artist, Böll feels it his task to remove

---

[1]"Heinrich Böll im Dialog: Klaus Harpprecht porträtiert Personen unserer Zeit," Sendung des ZDF am 6. 7. 1967.

[2]Heinrich Böll/Karen Struck, p. 64.

[3]*Ibid.*, p. 64.

"den Heiligen von der Wand und Wieder-zum-Leben-Bringen."[4] This was discussed in the previous chapter, where significant parallels were drawn between the medieval Saint Catherine of Siena and her contemporary counterparts Leni Pfeiffer and Katharina Blum. Böll, by reaching into history for his saintly model, reawakens her spirit for the modern world to experience.

Woman in Middle Ages

In his discussion with Karin Struck, Böll's familiarity with the religious movements predominant in the Middle Ages is discernable. He likens the hippie protest movement of the 1960's against "die totale hygienisierte zunächst amerikanische, dann europäische Gesellschaft,"[5] to the existent flagellant groups "und allen möglichen *pauperistischen* Bewegungen im Mittelalter."[6] Böll, in his depiction of woman and religion in *Gruppenbild mit Dame* and *Die verlorene Ehre Katharina Blum*, draws on a medieval historical model, that of a heresy known as the Catharist movement. So numerous are the parallels between the basic tenents of Catharism and the philosophy embraced by Böll in *Gruppenbild mit Dame* and *Katharina Blum*, that this similarity can surely not be fortuitous.

The role accorded woman in the Middle Ages can be summarized by two females, Eve and Mary. The clergy often repeated the story of biblical Eve, the sinful tempting woman, the "dirty matter" who betrayed God and man. She is delineated as "the gate of the devil, the traitor of the tree, the first deserter of Divine Law."[7] Every woman is depicted as Eve, the part of

---

[4]*Ibid.*, p. 64.

[5]*Ibid.*, p. 66.

[6]*Ibid.*, p. 66. "es waren ja ähnliche Protestbewegungen gegen eine saubere, etablierte, bürgerliche Gesellschaft." Catharism is the principal representative of the religious movements that advocated the primitive apostolic life, emphasizing poverty and asceticism (Briam Tierney, p. 315).

[7]Tertullian "De cultu feminarum," in *Patrologia Latina*, Volume I, Col. 1418-19.

man that is vulnerable to the temptations of the devil, the part responsible for his fall from grace. At the other extreme was the immaculate Virgin Mary, who was elevated to the status of a cult. This movement was at its height in the 11th century and remained such until the end of the Middle Ages.

According to the Church, woman was created "to preserve the species or to provide food and drink."[8] She was subjugated to the man. But on the other hand the Church and the aristocracy asserted with no sense of inconsistency the counter doctrine of the superiority of women as evidenced by the Virgin Mary cult.

The cult of the Virgin Mary and the cult of chivalry grew together, both reactions against the sombre realities of the Dark Ages. Pilgrimages were made to shrines of the Virgin, her miracles were recorded in books and manuscripts, and Saturdays were set aside for her worship.[9]

The romantic counterpart of this devotion of the Virgin Mary was found in the devotion bestowed upon a mortal lady. The lady was always married to someone else. The Knight served the lady as a vassal would serve a lord, performing knightly deeds and cultivating his knightly virtue. All virtue was considered grounded in love, love was considered to be the basis of literary perfection. Platonic love became a source of infinite spiritual possibilities. But this type of exaltation was the exclusive ideal of a small aristocratic caste. Essentially, woman was viewed as being inferior to man, as promulgated by the Church and its clergy.

Abelard, the medieval French scholastic philosopher (1079-1142), lamented the role accorded to woman by the Roman Church of the Middle Ages. Like Böll, Abelard reminded everyone of the fact that Christ's

---

[8]Friedrich Heer, *The Medieval World*, trans. Janet Sondheimer (New York: Mentor Books, 1962), p. 322.

[9]*Ibid.*, p. 322.

women disciples and friends stood closer to him than any of the men.[10] His resurrected body appeared to the women first, not to men. Abelard raised Mary Magdalene, the penitent saint, above the militant saints of the feudal Middle Ages, initiating thereby a Magdalene cult, a sort of spiritual eroticism.[11]

Abelard describes the men's minds of his time as being obsessed with power, honor, war and violence. According to Abelard, woman was refined in spirit and soul, "capable of conversing with God the Spirit in the inner kingdom of the soul on terms of intimate friendship."[12] He looked to woman as the new man,[13] a position Böll reiterated in elevating woman to the role of a "new Eve,"[14] a virginal, pure, and compassionate soul. Böll's ideal woman then is not a new creation, but an act of restoration, historical revival, of something that was lost. It is therefore most appropriate that he turned to a time in history when the Virgin cult originated and the role of woman was elevated as a result.

Abelard defended the much maligned woman of the Middle Ages, a task Böll sets for himself as an artist in his defense of the downtrodden, the outsiders of society. Böll feels that literature must choose as a subject matter, "was von der Gesellschaft zum Abfall, als abfällig erklärt wird...(p. 82) das von der Gesellschaft abfällig Behandelte in seiner Erhabenheit darzustellen."[15] He feels the humanity of a country "läßt sich

---

[10]Böll states in *Ansichten eines Clowns*: "Christus hat sozusagen privat fast nur mit Frauen Umgang gehabt."

[11]Heer, p. 114. "This can be seen depicted in the full flower of early Italian Renaissance art in the Bargello in Florence."

[12]Heer, p. 114.

[13]*Ibid.*, p. 114.

[14]Deschner, p. 11.

[15]*Frankfurter Vorlesungen*, p. 115.

daran erkennen, was in seinem Abfall landet, was an Alltäglichen, noch Brauchbarem, was an Poesie weggeworfen, der Vernichtung für wert erachtet wird."[16] Since Leni and Katharina are regarded by their contemporaries as "ausgediente Matratze" and "Kommunistensäue," or Abfall, he sets out to depict them in their "Erhabenheit."

Much like Abelard, who sought out the youth and women of medieval Europe, calling on them to think "boldly and to dare to love with passion, as befitted new man,"[17] Böll calls out to contemporary youth[18] to reevaluate the Church and society's dictates, and offers love as the only effective weapon to overcome the corruption in which we live. Böll's works then, in defense of Leni Pfeiffer and Katharina Blum, are vehicles of criticism against a smug materialistic society, much as the Catharist heresy was a mode of attack on the powerful medieval Roman Catholic Church.

Catharism

One of the principal reasons for the success of Catharism as a religious movement was the corrupt state of the priesthood during the 12th century.[19] Christ had preached against the dangers of worldly wealth. The religious were in theory forbidden to own property, but as the wealth of the higher clergy grew, the vows of apostolic poverty as well as non-political involvement in worldly affairs fell by the wayside. Abelard had seen the problem clearly and had recommended complete surrender of all property not absolutely necessary for the support of the clergy and the

---

[16]*Ibid.*, p. 115.

[17]Heer, p. 114.

[18]Heinrich Böll, *Brief an einen jungen Katholiken* (Cologne: Kiepenheuer and Witsch, 1961).

[19]Edmond Holmes, *The Albigensian of Catharist Heresy* (London: Williams and Norgate, Lte., 1925), p. 115.

cult.[20]

Many Christians in the 12th century were disturbed by the Clergy's open display of wealth and luxury.[21] Groups of zealous religious enthusiasts emphasizing poverty and asceticism split from the established Church. They were most vigorously opposed to violence of any kind and proclaimed war and the Crusades as sinful. The Cathar (the word *Cathari* comes from the Greek, meaning pure) movement was born out of this discontent with the established Church.

The movement spread between 1140 and 1160 from northern Europe southwards.[22] One of the early strongholds of the heresy was Cologne, the city that serves as the setting for all of Böll works. Böll, who has been dubbed the "arch Cologner among German writers of today,"[23] views Cologne's breed of Catholicism as "städtischer, freiheitlicher, than other old electorates and bishoprics whose faith he characterizes as "ergeben, ländlich, fast barock."[24]

Cologne has had a history of anticlericalism, "weil man Autorität nicht ernst nimmt."[25] Böll finds it ironic that the only cathedral left standing after the war and adapted for the coat of arms in Cologne was the Gothic Cologne Cathedral. He feels it is not at all representative of the

---

[20]Brian Tierney, Sidney Painter, *Western Europe in the Middle Ages 300-1475.* 2ndEdition. (New York: Alfred A. Knopf, 1974), p. 315.

[21]Böll attacks the modern Church and clergy for exactly the same type of greed and political involvement in temporal affairs. He feels they have become just one more pressure group lobbying for power.

[22]Wlater L. Wakefield, *Heresy, Crusade and inquisition in Southern France 1100-1250*, (Berkley: U. of California Press, 1974), p. 30.

[23]Leonhardt, p. 292.

[24]Heinrich Böll, "Der Rhein," in *Erzählungen Hörspiele Aufsätze* (Cologne: Kiepenheuer & Witch), p. 418.

[25]Heinrich Böll, "*Im Gespräch mit Heinz Arnold,*" p. 21.

117

religious reflection of Cologne, as Cologne Catholics have always been rebellious in nature.[26]

The Catharist movement penetrated Languedoc, an area of France, about 1150 and reached such proportions that a separate ecclesiastical council was held in 1167. Between 1150 and 1250 sixteen Catharist Churches organized as national groups. The movement reached its zenith of power at the end of the 12th century, beginning of the 13th century.

Under the protection of the cities, which enjoyed considerable freedom, and of the nobles, especially the Counts of Toulouse, the Cathars were free to practice their cult, to preach and hold councils.[27] Many of these powerful nobles were patrons of rich abbeys, which led to political conflicts with the bishops. The lesser nobles disputed with the monastaries over the division of tithes, contributing to the establishment of a nobility of heretics.[28] The Cathars became the "model of the Fronde and all reformist, enlightened and political resistance among the nobility down to nineteenth-century Russia because a new nobility had at last emerged."[29]

The basic doctrine of the Catharism was a theological dualism. According to the Catharists the good God created only the world of the spirit, the world of light. The bad God known to the Catharists as the

---

[26]There is an interesting and significant story about another one of Böll's favorite churches in Cologne, the Romanesque-Gothic church of St. Kolumba. It was totally destroyed by bombs during the war. The only thing remaining intact was a stone figure of the Madonna, which stood in an upright position, leaning against a 500 year old transept pillar. She became known to the Cologners as the *"Madonna of the Ruins,"* the only intact survivor among the rubble. An octagonal chapel was erected around her, symbolizing a truly contemporary house of God (Leonhardt, p. 292).

[27]Friedrich Heer, *The Intellectual History of Europe* (London: Weidenfield and Nicolson, 1966), transl: Jonathan Steinberg. Original published by W. Kohlhammer in 1953.

[28]*Ibid.*, p. 119.

[29]*Ibid.*, pp. 119-120.

Devil, created the visible, material world. The earth was regarded as a place of punishment and penitential suffering inhabited by fallen angels who followed the Devil. The Devil, governor of the earth, created the human body and is responsible for the moral evil in the world.

The aim of Catharism was to detach oneself by every possible means from the material world. The Catharists were not allowed to possess property, shed human blood for any purpose, kill animals or eat animal flesh. The purpose of human life was to free the soul from the prison of the body so that it could enter the kingdom of light after death. As the souls were redeemed the number of earthbound souls diminished. The Catharists therefore condemned marriage since it led to children and thus entrapped more spiritual souls in evil, material bodies. The soul must go through its purification in this world. If one lived too material a life, the soul would become too earthbound and be forced to come back to earth into some other living material body.

The Catharists consisted of two classes, the *perfecti* and the *credentes*. The *perfecti* constituted the priestly class, and were bound to lead the ideal life of rigid asceticism. The *credentes* (the believers) could live much as they liked, they could have families and also eat meat. To obtain a pardon for their sins they had to renounce their allegiance to the established Catholic church and receive the *consolamentum* before they died. The ceremony of the *consolamentum* combined baptism of the spirit, confirmation, priestly ordination and sometimes extreme unction all in one. When one received the *consolamentum*, one was free of the material world and the Devil, and was regarded as perfect, that is cleansed from sin. The great majority of believers postponed the consolamentum to the last moments of life, for if they recovered after having received the *consolamentum*, they had to lead the severely ascetic life of the *perfecti*.[30]

Those who aspired to an earlier baptism of the Holy Spirit were

[30]Edmond Holmes, pp. 24-29.

inducted into the class of *perfecti* through the *consolamentum*. They prepared themselves for admission to the priestly class, by participating in a one year novitiate, called the *Abstinentia*. During this period of preparation, the candidate lived in strict ascetism and utmost strictness under the guidance of a perfect. When deemed ready, the believer was presented to the assembled for the ceremony of the *consolamentum*. The ceremony was performed by two *perfecti*. It was a lengthy and formal ceremony. After confession and an exchange of prayers had taken place, the *perfecti* held an open Gospel over the candidate's head and all the other *perfecti* would place their hand upon his body in a laying-on-of-hands benediction. The ceremony ended with a kiss of peace. If the candidate was a woman the male perfectus was not allowed physical contact and would hold their hands above her, rather than on her.[31]

The perfect led a life of extreme severity. He, or she, ate no meat and drank no wine and observed three long fasts a year consisting of forty days each, living on bread and water alone. These *perfecti* wore a distinctive black costume and a leather bag containing a copy of the New Testament, traveled from place to place to preach, teach and administer the *consolamentum* to all deemed worthy. They led celibate lives, made vows of poverty and self-abnegation, and lived on bread, fish and fruit offered them by the believers, the *credentes*. Their ascetic life offered a striking contrast to the Catholic clergy who lived in luxury and whose conduct was often openly immoral. The *perfecti* were held in the utmost veneration by the believers, but their life demanded such ascetism that few could bear it. Around 1240 there were only 4,000 perfecti in the whole of Europe.[32]

The monthly religious ceremony of the Cathars, a rite known as the

---

[31]Holmes, pp. 24-26.

[32]Holmes, p. 27.

120

apparelliamentum or *servitium*, consisted of a public confession of the congregation to one of the *perfecti*. It was designed to renew the desire for transformation in souls. The believers were all required to participate "an dem Kernstück des katharischen Gottesdienstes, der sogenannten Brotbrechung."[33] A whole loaf is brought concealed in a white cloth. It is cut or broken and dispensed to all participants.[34] This rite was to be repeated daily by all believers at home before the meals. The Cathars used the words "supersubstantial bread" in lieu of "daily bread" in the Lord's Prayer because it is closer to the original Greek meaning.

Another common ceremony the Catharists attended was the *melioramentum*, a rite held to admire the *perfecti* by the believers. These services were usually held in "Schuppen, Kellern, Gelassen, in Wäldern und Waldhütten,"[35] because of the danger of being discovered and burned as heretics. Homage is actually paid to the Holy Spirit, which all men possess inside from the moment they enter the Catharist church. During the ceremony the Catharists express their desire to soon be among the ranks of the *perfecti*. Eleanor, the wife of Raymond VI of Toulouse, is reported to have conducted a solemn *melioramentum* secretly in the same chapel where the Pope was celebrating Mass.[36]

The organization of the Church was hierarchical in structure. The *perfecti* were considered the supreme caste, but there were bishops and deacons, whose duties were purely administrative. Each church had a bishop, and each bishop had a *filius major* and a *filius minor*, who replaced the bishop in his absence or in case of death.

Whereas the established Roman church relegated women to a

---

[33]Arno Borst, *Die Katharer* (Stuttgart: Hiersemann Verlag, 1953), p. 201.

[34]*Ibid.*, p. 201.

[35]*Ibid.*, p. 198.

[36]Heer, *The Medieval World*, p. 213.

secondary position in religion, the Catharists welcomed them to positions of leadership. There were no women among the Cathar bishops, for such a position was reserved for men who could endure the danger and fatigue of a wandering existence, but among the *credentes*, women exceeded men in numbers. Among the *perfecti*, there were fewer women than men, but not by a marked margin. Researchers of Deverneoy reveal that the number of women ordained as perfecti almost rivaled that of men until 1209.[37] Women *perfecti* were especially selected for their psychic gifts, and because of their capacity to emanate the spirit of goodness, hence they were called the *bonae Christianae*,[38] a name they earned. To heal was also a large part of the Cathar practice, for this reason it was fitting that many *perfecti* were women, for history had born out that the majority of those engaged in healing were women. The qualities of intuition, compassion and above all passivity ascribed to women, best qualified them to perform as agents of healing.[39] Faith-healing played an effective part in their cures, assuring them widespread fame and was thus responsible for dissemination of their beliefs. The women were more ardent in accepting Catharism as a faith, often encouraging their husbands to join. By the end of the 12th century, many noble ladies had turned over their homes and fortunes to the community to found Cathar convents, where daughters of aristocratic families and poor *credentes* found refuge. The great ladies in the area of Languedoc especially became fervent followers of Catharism. This can be in part accounted for by the greater degree of freedom the women of this area had enjoyed for more than a century. Respect for women had been

---

[37]Arthur Guirdham, *The Great Heresy* (Jersey: Neville Spearman, 1977), p. 14.

[38]These women conducted the apostolate among women *credentes*. They were concerned with their education and acted as doctors and nurses. Many devoted themselves to the contemplative life, more so than was the case among their male counterparts (*bons hommes*). Oldenbourg, p. 61.

[39]Guirdham, p. 39.

compelled by the Provencial literature, where the tradition of *amour courtois* originated. Women were often better educated than their husbands and were allowed to own property in their own right, yet in the eyes of the Catholic Church they remained second-class citizens.

Catharism, in allowing women into the ranks of the priestly class, recognized woman as man's equal. Once she had received the Holy Spirit, she was able to transmit this Spirit by a laying-on-of-hands "though as a rule they only did so in cases of emergency, and far less frequently than men."[40] Women *perfecti* were often regarded virtually as the Mother Superior of the particular community. Blanche de Laurac ran a convent for Catharist women with her daughter Mabylia. She belonged to one of the most powerful feudal families of Southern France and serves as evidence of the zealous following that the Catharists had in that class of society. Women often lived in grottos or huts in "klosterähnlichen Gruppen zusammen."[41]

> Alle sind einander in *herzlicher Gemeinschaft verbunden,* denn über ihnen, die 'mit traurigem Gesicht und tränenreicher Stimme' *durch die böse Welt gehen, liegt die stille Freude der Auserwählten, die das Irdische überwunden haben*[42] (Emphasis added).

One of the most well known female *perfecti* was Esclarmonde de Foix, who was recognized for many years as the most holy of all the Cathar women.[43] She was the widowed sister of the Count of Foix. She

---

[40]Zoe Oldenbourg, *Massacre at Montsegur* (New York: George Weidenfeld & Nicolson, Ltd., 1961), p. 61.

[41]Borst, p. 207.

[42]*Ibid.*, p. 207.

[43]Sir Steven Runciman, *The Medieval Manichee* (Cambridge: Cambridge U. Press, 1960).

often took part in debates between Cathar and Catholic preachers. During one of these debates in her brother's castle of Pamiers, her intervention was cut short by a monk who told her: "Go madame, spin at your distaff. You know nothing of such matters."[44] This attitude displayed by the monk reflects the position of the Catholic Church at large.

Esclarmonde of Foix enjoyed great success in making a number of conversions. She was so influential that she received special dispensation to eat meat and tell lies when necessary.[45] When she received the *consolamentum* in 1505, the ceremony was attended by her brother, the Count, and most of the nobility of the county.[46]

Many of the Catharist convents were broken up by the Inquisition led by the Roman Church. Many women flocked to Montsegur during these troubled times and it remained the final stronghold of the Cathars. Numerous huts were built by them on the mountainside, which were almost totally inaccessible. Montsegur was forced to capitulate on March 1, 1244. During the fifteen day truce that ensued, several persons received the *consolamentum*, among them the wife of the seigueir of Montsegur, Corba de Perella. She abandoned her husband, two daughters, son and grandchildren for self-martyrdom for the faith she held.[47] About 200 *perfecti* were burned at the stake as heretics: "the martyrs of a defeated creed never achieve canonization, but these men and women . . . richly deserve to be remembered as true martyrs."[48] With the defeat at Montsegur, the believers were either executed or so scattered that the heresy is not mentioned again. It has, however, enjoyed a recent revival in

---

[44]Vaissete-Molinier, *Historie du Languedoc*, Vol. VIII, p. 224.

[45]Oldenbourg, p. 275.

[46]Vaissete-Molinier, *Historie de Languedoc*, preuves, no. 263.

[47]Oldenbourg, p. 360.

[48]*Ibid.*, p. 361.

the south of France, bringing with it much new literature and information about the medieval cult.

Catharism and Böll: Parallels

Much light has been shed on the role of Catharism in the 20th century by Jean Michel Angebert[49] in an interesting study entitled *The Occult and the Third Reich.*[50] The authors link Hitler and National Socialism with medieval Cathar thought and practices. Angebert finds "Nazism is only the most recent outcropping of a militant neo-Paganism locked in a death struggle with its arch enemy, traditional Christianity, a struggle which will go on to the end of time."[51] The author views this struggle as a constant confrontation between underground occult forces.[52] It seems almost grotesquely ironic that the same movement could have stimulated two such opposite people as Hitler and Böll. Actually, the Angebert study shows Hitler's fascination with Catharism to have issued from the elitest premise of the organization and its claim to an ideological descent from the Aryan race. Böll inspiration is quite dissimilar.

Böll in discussing the interpretation of his novels, has given critics the following important clue: "Ein Roman . . . ist ein Versteck, in dem man zwei, drei Worte verstecken kann, von denen man hofft, daß der Leser sie findet."[53] It is the concluding contention of this study that one of the hidden words and a key to a new interpretation in Böll works is the name Katharina--coming from the Greek word Καπηαροσ, meaning pure,

[49]Jean-Michel Angebert is the joint signature of Michel Bertrand & Jean Angeline, two French scholars whose research of mystical cults has been extensive.

[50]Jean-Michel Angebert, *The Occult and the Third Reich* trans. Lewis A.M. Sumbert (New York: McGraw-Hill, 1975).

[51]*Ibid.*, p. XIX.

[52]*Ibid.*, p. XIX.

[53]Horst Bienek, "Heinrich Böll," in *Werkstattgespräche mit Schriftstellern* (Munich: Hanser Verlag, 1962), p. 143.

referring directly to the group in history who called themselves the pure ones, the Cathars.

The principal tenets of Catharism overlap to a remarkable degree the themes in Böll works. As we have seen in tracing the development of women figures, Böll's first literary efforts dealt almost exclusively with the senselessness of war (*Wo warst du Adam, Der Zug war pünktlich*) and its devastating aftermath (*Und sagte kein einziges Wort, Haus ohne Hüter, Billard um halbzehn*). The Cathars condemned all violence, they viewed war and the Crusades as sins.[54] "Even their worst enemies testify that they never encouraged their faithful to violence against their adversaries."[55] A soldier who killed an enemy in battle or a judge who condemned a criminal to death were as culpable as murderers and assassins.[56]

Böll criticism moves to an attack on the immediate postwar era and the *Wirtschaftswunder*. His social criticism is primarily aimed at a society which is only concerned with prosperity and which has successfully repressed the events of the recent past as if they had not occurred. Böll fears a repetition of the same errors, if full responsibility is not accepted for the past. His bitterest satire is hurled at the *dicke Fresser*, the *Konsumgesellschaft*, and the *Büffel* who selfishly forge ahead regardless of the suffering they cause others. Böll draws a parallel between the *Büffel* and the Nazis in the evils they perpetrated and still perpetrate, underscoring the repetitive danger of these evils.

Böll sets up a Manichean division between the *Büffel* and the

---

[54]Borst, "Der Gebrauch des Schwertes zu Krieg und Kreuzzug ist Sünde...die Strafvollstreckung ist die Sache Gottes, nicht des Papstes oder Kaisers" (p. 187).

[55]Jacques Madaule, *The Albigensian Crusade* transl. by Barbara Wall. (New York: Fordham U. Press, 1967) p. 55. *Le Drame albigeois et le Destin français*, Bernard Grasset Editeuer, Paris, 1961.

[56]Edmond Holmes, p. 23.

Lämmer which is analagous to the Cathars' dualistic view of good and evil. The lambs, according to Böll (the good) are figures of innocence, who are often a political and non-conformist in their defiance to comply with the material world. They are selfless in their love for their fellow man and become the victims of a predatory society. The buffaloes (the evil) are the opportunists, materialists, whose self-interest rules their every action. They function well in the army, politics and the Church, all three of which institutions are vehemently opposed by the Cathars. As was indicated earlier, one reason Catharism began as a religion was because of its open criticism of the Church's involvement in temporal and political affairs, "Das Reich und die Nationen sind den Katharen feind."[57] The Church was vying for political power with politically powerful nobles, forgetting its Christian mission of the salvation of souls.

The Cathars, the pure ones, like the *Lämmer*, were non-conformists, apolitical figures of innocence, who led a simple life, "sie folgten dort noch den christlichen Lebensregeln der *Bescheidenheit, Demut und Wahrheitsliebe.*"[58] They depended wholly on the *credentes* for food, clothing and shelter. The female *credentes* were more instrumental in performing these duties than their male counterparts.[59] It is interesting to note that Böll assigns this task of ministering to the needs of others almost exclusively to women. The *Mädchen* (*Und sagte kein einziges Wort*) is the prime example of this type of *Engelfigur*, whose selfless love forces her to minister to the needs of others. Like the *perfecti*, the *Mädchen* "demonstrated what men who lived by 'pure spirit' could achieve."[60] Both figures are reminiscent of the "Holy Fools" from the Epistle of St. Paul,

---

[57]Borst, p. 226.

[58]*Ibid.*, p. 203.

[59]Oldenbourg, p. 61.

[60]Heer, *The Medieval World*, p. 210.

who have attained such purity of spirit that they have achieved liberation from the evil world and from matter, the goal of Catharism.

The corrupt state of the priesthood when Catharism challenged the Catholic Church was one of the reasons for its success as a proselytizing religion. The immorality and worldliness of the Catholic clergy was of great concern to its members because they doubted the efficaciousness of a sacrament administered by a priest who was living in open sin. In the administration of their own sacrament, the *consolamentum*, the person administering the sacrament must be pure of heart,[61] the outward act was purely symbolic, the prayer alone mattered.

The Cathar ceremony of the *consolamentum* enjoys several parallels to the *Handauflegung* scene between Leni and Boris. As was mentioned earlier, the women *perfecti* usually administered the consolamentum only in times of emergency. Böll described the external circumstances surrounding Leni and Boris as a "höchst schwierige Situation."[62] Böll chooses a woman perfect to perform the ceremony of the *consolamentum*. He thus endows woman with the power to impart the Holy Spirit to man by a laying-on-of-hands: "durch bloßes Handauflegen versetzte sie den Sowjetmenschen in Glückseligkeit." Once a *credentes* becomes a *perfecti*, according to the Cathars, he or she is allowed to recite the Lord's Prayer, one of two prayers Leni knows by heart and enjoys reciting. Because Böll has accorded woman the ability to perform this benediction, perhaps he sees in her alone the "pureness of heart" required to administer this sacrament. From her nature alone, woman's "Hände" perform acts of love and compassion.

Many critics have written about Böll symbolic use of bread. A loaf of bread is most often depicted as being offered by a woman to a soldier

---

[61]Holmes, p. 118.

[62]Böll/Wellershoff, p. 337.

returning from war. In giving him the bread she illustrates her compassion and understanding and gives him new spiritual as well as physical life. In discussing the function of bread in his works, Böll stated:

> Was ich gern entwickeln würde: eine *Aesthetik des Brotes*, das zuerst das reale, vom Bäcker oder von der Hausfrau, vom Bauern gebackene ist, doch auch mehr, viel *mehr* -- *Zeichen der Brüderlichkeit* nicht nur, auch des Friedens, sogar der Freiheit, und wiederum noch mehr: das wirkungsvollste Aphrodisiakum und weiterhin: Hostie, Oblate, Mazze, magisch verwandelt zur Pille, die ihre Form von der Hostie hat, Ersatz ist für Brüderlichkeit Frieden, Freiheit, Aphrodisiakum.[63]

Central to the religious service of the Cathars was the breaking of the bread ceremony. The bread, as described above, was a complete loaf of bread, broken up and distributed to all participants. This breaking of the "supersubstantial" bread had to be repeated by all Cathars at least once a day. They consumed their daily bread with the same sense of routine that Leni consumed her beloved *Brötchen*, "den grössten Wert legt Leni auf die frischen Bötchen, (p. 11)." The meticulous way in which she consumed her daily bread is described like a ceremony by Böll, which indeed it is to Leni. For Leni her daily consumption of bread replaces the need for the communion host in a church. The host itself is tasteless and dry, which she wishes only to expel, unlike the baker's bread, of which she is careful to gather every crumb. The Cathars, of course, did not believe that the communion host turned into the actual blood and body of Christ, but did attach an almost metaphysical meaning to it. During the times of persecution, when the *perfecti* were in hiding, the *Brotbrechung* took place on special religious holidays only, "fragments of the bread so blessed were then carried by faithful messengers to the towns and villages and

---

[63]Böll, *Frankfurter Vorlesungen*, p. 97.

distributed among believers, who carefully preserved them in caskets, sometimes for years at a time."[64] Leni, who would be verbally accosted during her daily walk to the bakery, risked persecution in making the trip herself. In speaking of women's vs. men's hands in *Ansichten eines Clowns*, Böll uses the image of a woman spreading butter on bread as a description of loving hands which are "fast keine Hände mehr." The men are always the recipients of such loving gestures.

The healing ability, allegedly possessed by the *perfecti*, was a type of faith healing. Women often served as doctors and nurses, as healing ministers. The beliefs of the Cathars spread successfully in large part due to the miracle cures that allegedly occurred. Leni herself is depicted as a spiritual healer in *Gruppenbild mit Dame*, both by raising Boris to the level of *Mensch*, and by giving even the opportunistic Pelzer a soul: *"Ich spüre zum erstenmal, daß ich eine Seele habe* und diese Seele leidet, zum erstenmal erlebe ich, daß nicht irgendeine, *nur eine Frau mir helfen kann"* (p. 367 emphasis added). In his early works, a character such as Pelzer would have remained a totally negative person, e.g. Gäseler and Frau Francke, but Böll's Manichean depiction of his characters ends through the contact with the pureness of Leni Pfeiffer. Leni is also capable of physical healing, as evidenced by the miraculous curing of her little boy's wound to which she applied her saliva: *"Sie heilte nicht nur den Sowjetmenschen und ihren Sohn mit Speichel, durch bloßes Handauflegen versetzte sie den Sowjetmenschen in Glückseligkeit und beruhigte sie ihren Sohn* (p. 33)."

The quality of compassion is best seen in Leni's closest companion, Margret, whom Böll dubbed "die allzu barmherzige Samariterin." If she could bring a moment of happiness to others, she gave of herself freely to "jedem, der nett aussah und traurig drein blickte, voll Barmherzigkeit." The main criterion for *perfecti* then are clearly visible in Böll's positive women characters.

---

[64]Holmes, p. 34.

The only prayers that Leni knows are the The Lord's Prayer and the Ave Maria. In the Catharist religions, only the *perfecti, die Vollendeten,* are allowed to offer the Lord's prayer:

> Nur die Vollendeten dürfen das Vaterunser beten, denn es ist der Lobgesang der Engel im Himmel gewesen, bei ihrem Fall haben sie es vergessen, bis Christus kam und es sie wieder lehrt. Darum wird auch die 'übergabe des Vaterunser,' die tradition orationis dominicae, zum ersten Akt der feierlichen Aufnahmezeremonie ausgestaltet.[65]

Leni is depicted as the *Vollendete* who is viewed as a priest, an example to her followers. The prayer of the followers is a simple one in which they express their desire to be *Vollendete* themselves someday: "Herr, wie Du die drei Könige geleitet hast, so leite auch mich!"[66] The basic hierarchy of the Catharist church thus provides a key to an interpretation of Böll *Gruppenbild mit Dame.*

Upon receiving the *consolamentum* the new *Vollendete* is told by his fellow *perfecti,* that through this *Geistestaufe* he has become a member of the Catharist Church and is *"in der Welt wie das Schaf inmitten von Wölfen."*[67] This statement holds true for Böll's *Lämmer* figures as well. He simply changes the word *Wölfe* to *Büffel.* Kate, Edith, Leni, and Katharina are the *Lämmer,* the victims of the *Büffel.* Leni's followers, or *Gemeinschaft,* provide protection for her, much as the *credentes* did for the *perfecti.* Her first community of followers consisted of her fellow workers at Pelzer's wreath factory. They silently swore never to betray her or her relationship with Boris. The *perfecti,* like Leni, had to retreat to

[65]Borst, p. 192.

[66]*Ibid.,* p. 192.

[67]Anselmus de Alexandria O.P. *Tractatus de haereticitis.* Ausgabe: Dondaine, Italie 308-324.

"Schuppen, Keller, and *Unterirdische Gelasse*" to hold their *Gottesdienst*. The *perfecti* and believers often met at night, as Leni and Boris had to meet during the air raids in order to prevent discovery and execution.

Leni's second community of believers consisted of ostracized members of society (*Abfall*), by whom she was regarded as "eine Mantelmadonna Schutz...(sie) wird Stütze und Zuflucht für ihre Zeugen, die sich in einer immer grösseren Zahl um sie scharen."[68] This is reminiscent of the mass flocking of women *credentes* to Montsegur during the Inquisition, seeking to protect the last stronghold of Catharism and Corba de Perella, the wife of the Seigneur of Montsegur. At that time the number of female credentes outnumbered the male credentes. This also holds true in *Gruppenbild mit Dame*, Leni's female followers outnumber the male followers 6 to 2 in the wreath factory and her closest friends and mentors are all women: Margret, Rahel, Lotte, and Marja von Doorn.

The purely administrative positions within the Catharist Church, the bishops and deacons, were solely filled by males. This would be in agreement with Böll's view of men as he states they possess "Sinn für Organisation und den ganzen Unsinn" (*Ansichten eines Clowns*).

Many of the noble women Cathars were intellectuals in their own right. Their only refuge had been the convent to pursue their intellectual activities, but Catharism offered them an active role in the Church. It is interesting to note that all of the intellectual women in Böll novels are nuns or former nuns, and their intellectual pursuits were in fields regarded as permissable for women in the convents in the Middle Ages. Ilona (*Wo warst du Adam?*) studied *Germanistik* and music and was a teacher. She, like many female *credentes*, becomes a martyr by choice, much like Corba de Perella, and is a victim of religious persecution. Rahel, (*Gruppenbild mit Dame*), a Jewish convert to Catholicism like Ilona, was a physician, who enjoyed philosophy as well. She is persecuted by her fellow nuns and

---

[68]Bernath, p. 53.

society and also dies a martyr's death. Her association with the Virgin Mary is revealed in the miracle that occurs after her death. Klementina (*Gruppenbild mit Dame*) has been a nun for many years, her field of scholarship is 20th century German literature. The description of the convent with its tall walls and isolation is the same as one from the Middle Ages. Perhaps Böll is hinting that the role of the intellectual woman has not progressed much further either. All of these women possess occupations where they minister to the needs of others (teacher, physicians). Ilona and Klementina leave the convent in pursuit of love and happiness. The war does not allow Ilona's dream to be fulfilled, but Klementina may secure happiness with the *Verf.* Rahel, in her death, is raised to a suggestion of sainthood. Her spirit lives on in Leni.

The Cathars held that the Virgin Mary was an angel "durch dessen Ohr Christus einging in diese Welt, begabt mit einem Scheinleib ohne irdische Materie."[69] It is interesting to compare this with Böll's depiction of Leni. The *Verf.* goes through much effort to prove that Leni and Boris could not have been together the day Lev was conceived, because there was no air raid on that day, implying thereby an immaculate conception.

Like Böll, the Cathars glorified the artisans, "die ersten Katharer schlossen sich dieser Hochschätzung der *Handarbeit* an und verdienten sich ihren Lebensunterhalt durch eigene Anstrengung."[70] In Böll's choice of professions for his positive male figures, all are either artisans or are gifted with a skill that involves use of the hands. Andreas is a pianist, Feinhals, an architect, Albert, a caricaturist, Walter Fendrich, a machine repairman, Hans, a mime artist and clown, Robert Fähmel, an architect, Georg Gruhl, a carpenter, Boris, a street engineer, and the *Verf.*, a journalist. Many of them possess tools of their trades, such as brushes,

---

[69]Borst, p. 163.

[70]*Ibid.*, p. 188.

rulers, pencils, compasses. Their female counterparts are either mothers and wives, and involved in everyday life, or they are intellectuals in the literary, scientific or philosophical realm. Their tools in life are those of love and compassion. They bestow this love on others, especially on their men, whom they nourish both physically and spiritually.

Böll's women figures seem to draw out the good in man (Olina, Ilona, Käte, Katharina Mirzow, Leni); as loving and compassionate beings they bring the straying man back (Hedwig, Käte, Katharina Mirzow) and help expiate his sins with their prayers (Käte Bogner). In Böll, man turns to woman to find a deeper significance in his own existence, women become an intermediary between God and man through love, their physical beauty attracts man and God is moved through their prayers, much as the Virgin Mary is an intermediary between man and God.

The role of woman in Böll's early fiction was a passive one. She worked behind the scenes as mother and wife, and through prayer, provided a link with God (*Kinder, Küche, Kirche*). When her role of wife and mother was usurped during and after the war, and the Church no longer provided a sanctuary for her, she was forced to seek new goals and to face new challenges. She is depicted as a lamb and becomes a victim of society and of the *Büffel* (Käte, Wilma Brielach). The first attempt at an active offense against the oppressors is made by Johanna Fähmel, marking the end in Böll of withdrawal as a possible solution to the evils of society. Johanna's individual protest is soon followed by a united effort on the part of *Abfallfahrer*[71] in defense of Leni Pfeiffer. She becomes the model of virtue who inspires humanity in others. With the appearance of Katharina Blum, the shot fired by Johanna Fähmel finds its mark. Katharina Blum's *Rufmord* by a journalist does not force her to retreat. She is no longer

---

[71]It is interesting to note that Böll chooses "Abfallfahrer" to protect Leni, thus underscoring once more his statement made in the *Frankfurter Vorlesungen* (1963/64, II, 71) "Die Literatur kann offenbar nur zum Gegenstand wählen, was von der Gesellschaft zum *Abfall, als abfällig erklärt wird*" (Emphasis added).

delineated as the victim, for she chooses to act. By doing away with the perpetrator of evil, Katharina is rewarded by feeling neither regret nor guilt. In silent recognition of her actual innocence, she receives a mild legal sentence. She not only survives as does Leni, "fast unverletzt," she bounces back more determined than before to plan for the future.

Chapter Six

Das Ewig Weibliche

In the novel, *Fürsorgliche Belagerung*, it is not surprising, in viewing Böll's opus as a *Fortschreibung*,[1] to find the names of the major women figures to be Katharina. Indeed in this novel, Böll goes so far as to use three variations in three generations of that very name: Käthe, Katharina and Kit, thus once more underscoring the "pure" side of their nature.

Böll's positive women show the traditional womanly traits of compassion, innocence and are deeply religious.[2] In Böll's view "sind es die Frauen, denen die Verwirklichung des Menschseins in der Einheit von Leib, Seele und Geist gelingt und die dadurch sensibel für das Leben sind."[3] In his earlier works, Böll depicted a love relationship in a war-time setting or an equally oppressive restorative society. This novel is a continuation of that theme. Fritz recalls when he was a soldier, and Käthe, a nurse; during the war. This scene is reminiscent of the scene between Andreas and Olina in *Der Zug war pünktlich*.[4]

> Er (Fritz) blickte auf sie herunter, eine Blonde, mit offenem Gesicht, ein bißchen pummelig, *graue verschleierte Augen im Widerspruch zu der offenen Heiterkeit ihres Gesichts, Augen, aus denen er nie mehr*

---

[1]Böll expressed that his work should be viewed and understood as "vorläufiges Ergebnis" of an epic "Fortschreibung" (*Frankfurter Vorlesungen* 1963/64, IV, p. 120).

[2]This religion, it must be noted, is not an institutionalized religion, based on ritual and formalism, but an internal one. This is made clear in that Böll's women find no consolation in confession to a priest, but in prayer.

[3]Manfred Nielen. *Frömmigkeit bei Heinrich Böll*. Annweiler: Thomas Pröger Verlag, 1987. p. 80.

[4]"die sanften trauigen Augen...sie blickten sich lange an, sehr lange an, sehr lange, und ihre Augen versinken ineinander." (*Der Zug war pünktlich*, pp. 107-108).

herauskommen wollte, sollte, blickte so intensiv, daß sie noch einmal errötete. (p. 139)[5]

Like Andreas, Fritz upon meeting Käthe, casts all fear aside:

> er wollte bei ihr bleiben, in ihre Augen und nicht nur in ihre Augen sehen, er wollte sie haben, behalten und sagte es ihr. (p. 141)

He takes her home to her father, away from "wo es 'nur Nazis und Protestanten gab'" (p. 141).

In his description of Käthe, Böll once more characterizes her by using the eyes as a measure. In comparing her eyes with the eyes of her son Rolf: "Ihre waren ein weniger heller, nur einen winzingen Schimmer heller, und doch halten sie auch *diese Dimension poetischer Trauer,* nur flüchtig getarnt von einer Leichtfertigkeit, hinter der sich Verzweiflung verbarg" (p. 116). This dimension of "poetischer Trauer" is lacking in Fritz. He, as a businessman, has sacrificed the sense of poetic abandoning that Käthe and Rolf possess. Once he is firmly entrenched in the business world, Käthe alone is able to offer him consolation no one else can, serving as a reminder of "seine offene, fast schon aktenkundige Menschlichkeit" (p. 131). Käthe is able to sustain him spiritually to persevere and tolerate his existence. She serves as a guide to her husband, innately knowing his real needs and desires. She advises him early in their married life to become a museum director "Kultusminister oder wenigstens Kulturdezerent" (p. 116), but Fritz possesses a drive for success and money that masks his real desires.

Fritz Tolm has recently been elected president of a newspaper union. As a V.I.P., he must be protected and guarded from attempts on his life. As all of Böll's heroes, the resulting intricate police security network leads to

---

[5]Heinrich Böll, *Fürsorgliche Belagerung* (Cologne: Kiepenheuer and Witch, 1979), p. 139.

total isolation from the world resulting in a very oppressive environment. The only private refuge offered Fritz and Käthe is under an umbrella on the veranda, much like the vault of Leni and Boris (*Gruppenbild mit Dame*). It is, however, also bugged, and Fritz and Käthe must resort to writing down their endearments on paper and flushing them down the toilet.

Unlike Fritz, Käthe survives this oppressive life relatively unscathed, and succeeds in leading a somewhat normal life. She, much like Leni and Katharina before her, is compassionate toward those in need, providing both spiritual and material nourishment to those around her. The women, as typical of Böll, are depicted as "die frommen Menschen . . . weil für ihn echte Frömmigkeit fest und bruchlos mit dem ganzen Leben des Menschen verknüpft sein muß."[6] It is public knowledge that Käthe is doing very "suspect" things, but her motivation is never called into question by any of the narrators. Holzpuke, the chief of the security guards, says of her: "man mußte auf sie achtgeben, zu ihrem eigenen Heil, sie hatte eine etwas zu lockere Hand -- nicht nur für Illegales, das mußte vermerkt werden. Sie unterstützte viele Leute" (p. 359). This is very reminiscent of Katharina Blum and Leni Pfeiffer, whose motivation of compassion far outweigh all thoughts of riches or ownership. Käthe is loved by all, even her supposed enemies, such as Bleibl. In time of need she is the only person he feels he can talk to about the guilt of a crime he committed many years ago: "Vielleicht war Käthe Tolm die einzige Person, mit der er über seine Leiche im Keller, über seine Einsamkeit sprechen konnte" (p. 334). Her compassion for her *Mitmenschen* overcomes all barriers.

Katharina Schröter, Käthe and Fritz Tolm's daughter-in-law, displays very similar traits of compassion and generosity. She is Böll's most touching and warm woman figure in this novel. Her entire being radiates warmth that Fritz describes as

---

[6]Nielen, p. 80.

eine Wärme . . . wie er es nur bei sich selbst so nannte (nie
würde er das äußern, nie auch nicht auf der Schiene der
Zweibahnigkeit) *'kommunistische Wärme'* die ihn an
Kommunisten seiner Kindheit und Jugend erinnerte, . . .
an den einzigen Thälmann-Wähler, der so gut mit
Kindern umgehen konnte, daß er den Ruf eines
Rattenfängers geraten war" (p. 59).

Katharina's spontaneous love and generosity allow her to touch the lives
of those around her and gain adherents much like Leni Pfeiffer. Like Leni,
Katharina can make an intolerable life meaningful and tolerable. She and
her adherents eventually form an alternative society. They are able to
bring out the good in those close to them. Rolf had been an active violent
protester against the capitalistic society, but once Katharina's "Wärme"
touched him he was transformed as seen in Fritz' description while
witnessing a family scene:

> Es war so eine undurchsichtige, von merkwürdiger
> Trauer umschattete Dimension in seinen Augen, eine
> Dimension, die undurchdringlich blieb, dichter wurde,
> wenn er mit seinem kleinen Sohn Holger spielte . . . mit
> einer so fremden kühlen Zärtlichkeit und Trauer . . . auch
> wenn er Katharina ansah, in flüchtiger Zärtlichkeit, das
> Berühren ihrer Hand, wenn er ihr Feuer gab oder eine
> Tasse von ihr entgegennahm, das war Welten entfernt
> von der Schlüpfrigkeit, mit der Kohlschröder solche
> Gesten ausführt" (p. 59).

The only time Fritz is overcome with feelings, or emotion is upon contact
with Katharina's spontaneous gestures of kindness. As Leni was able to
make Boris a human in front of all by offering a 'chalice' of coffee, so
Katharina's smile accomplishes the same end. Only Fritz finds solace:
"diese Ruhe, die man bei Rolf und Katharina noch finden konnte" (p. 171).
Fritz is surprised by her warmth:

"Mein Gott, Vater"--ja, sie nannte ihn Vater! "was stehst
du denn hier wie ein Ausgestoßener, komm doch rein, du
störst doch nicht, störst doch nie"--*und ihm waren fast
die Tränen* gekommen, weil sie so nett war, ihn Vater
nannte, ihn beim Arm nahm und an diesem neblig trüben
Novemberabend in die Wohnung führt" (p. 167).

The consolation she is able to provide by her presence alone, triggers an emotional note in Fritz he simply cannot explain:

eine junge Frau, wie alle anderen mit roten, langen
Strümpfen, losem Haar, und als sie ihr erblickte, hatte er
dieses plötzliche, auflechtende Lacheln, *daß ihm wieder
einmal die Tränen zu kommen drohten* . . . Sie hatte ihn
doch ganz offensichtlich gern: *dieses plötzliche Lächeln
auf ihrem Gesicht* da draußen auf der Straße . . . *Er hatte
keine Mühe, sie sich als Nonne vorzustellen* -- und doch
waren ihre Klugheit Sensibilität und Intelligenz auf
dieses Dorf beschränkt (p. 169).

Katharina Blum's nickname was "Nonne," because of her prudishness toward the advances of "zudringliche" men. Fritz can easily envision Katharina Schröter as a nun as well. It is interesting to note that Böll, in his earlier works, offered the monastery as a solution to one's inability to cope with a society, whose ideals and morality were not acceptable (*Nicht nur zur Weihnachtszeit*). In the progression of his opus, Böll criticizes the monks for outwardly supporting the Nazis (*Ansichten eines Clowns*); in *Gruppenbild mit Dame*, Klementina, who had been in a convent for eighteen years, chooses to return to the world, but she is equipped with intelligence, a profession and a man to share her ideals. Böll increasingly advocates an active participation by the *Lämmer* in the world. He continues to espouse this philosophy in the characters of Käthe and Katharina in *Fürsorgliche Belagerung*.

As the novel progresses, more and more people turn to Rolf and Katharina for moral and spiritual support. Their small dwelling is depicted as a paradise, open to all, where no secrets prevail and their lives are an open book. It has replaced Eickelhof, the "lost paradise," as a retreat where a little "Ruhe" can still be found. When Fritz's mansion is destroyed by fire, he and Käthe, too, will turn to Rolf and Katharina's alternative society.

It is interesting that all characters, minor and major, are involved in a love relationship, underscoring Böll's contention that at the center of his work is the relationship between a man and a woman.[7] These pairings are Fritz/Käthe; Katharina/Rolf; Veronika/Beverloh; Sabine/Hubert; Monka/Karl; Erna/Peter; Helga/Hubert; and Eva/Blurtmehl. All relationships are strained as a result of their association with, or to Fritz Tolm and his family members.

Eva-Marie Magdalena

Among the women figures, Böll does not neglect his favorite woman character, the Magdalena figure. In *Fürsorgliche Belagerung* the most outstanding Magdalena figures are Erna, Monka and the unforgettable Gerlinde: "Dieses Mädchen, das als 'frech' and 'verdorbenes Luder' galt, war sanft geworden auch still, schon atemlose, und die verrückte Freude auf ihrem Gesicht, dieses Glück, daß er fast Seligkeit nennen mochte, -- vergaß er nicht, nie, und nicht ihr Lächeln über seine Freude" (p. 28). Böll regards these women as true *Freudenmädchen*, not *Huren* oder *leichtfertige Frauen*--he even asks "warum sprachen sie dann nicht endlich die Gerlinde heilig" (p. 30)?

Böll does not neglect the Eva side in his latest novel. In fact, Böll even names her *Eva* Klensch. She is a striking beauty, desired by all who see her, even the meek Fritz Tolm himself: "er fragte sie nach ihrem Beruf, dann ihren Geschäften, bewunderte ihren Mut, ihren Unternehmungsgeist und hatte Angst, ihr wirklich tief in die Augen zu sehen" (p. 200). She is very much an intellectual, interested especially in art and art history. She is

---

[7]Böll/Wellershoff, p. 337.

most reminiscent of Katharina Blum in that she is a self-actualized woman, able to fulfill her physical needs (hunger, thirst, sex), her security needs (shelter, protection) and her social needs (affection, love).[8] She is described as "eine hübsche, selbstsichere, geschäftstüchtige junge Frau, die geschickt und *völlig legal* die schwankenden Dollarkurse ausnutzte..."(p. 12). She accomplishes her success through legal means and hard work, not by being shrewd and calculating. She is still very much depicted as a loving and compassionate woman.

The only negative woman in this novel is Edelgard, the fourth wife of Bleibl. Käthe had characterized her as "ein dummes Luder" and Bleibl concurs:

> diese künstliche Sinnlichkeit, heiseres Geflüsters aus blöden Filmen abgeguckt...ein dummes Luder, vielleicht ein armes Luder, das sogar dumme Hände hatte...die offenbar ohne Musik nicht leben konnte (pp. 318-19).

She revels in the security awarded her, viewing it as a sign of prestige, rather than an invasion of her privacy. She is depicted as very superficial, concerned only with the externals of success and power.

In his last and final work written before his death on July 16, 1985, *Frauen vor Flußlandschaft*, Böll gives credence to the role of woman in the title alone. Women are depicted as "menschlich ausgeprägte Charaktere"[9] unlike the men in the novel. The women are endowed with wisdom and insight as well as intelligence, "jedoch ist keine von ihnen so profoliert wie etwa Leni Pfeiffer in *Gruppenbild*."[10]

As in his three previous major works, the names Böll accords these women (Eva, Katharina, Elisabeth and Erika) is significant and offers the

---

[8]Abraham Maslow. *Toward a Psychology of Being* (Princeton: Van Nostrand, 1962).

[9]Henning Falkenstein. *Heinrich Böll*. Berlin: Colloquium Verlag, 1987, p. 78.

[10]Ibid. p. 78.

reader insight into the characters. As previously noted, Böll defines the tension that exists in woman by three names: "Eva, Maria, Magdalena, die sich nie rein, nie getrennt zeigen in der weiblichen Natur."[11] By investigating the origin of the names, these three aspects of the *Trinität des Weiblichen* become visible. The name Erika comes from the Greek word meaning "heather" (*Heidekraut*), a conscious allusion to Leni Pfeiffer's *Heidekrauterlebnis*, her first sexual experience at the age of sixteen, alluding to the Virgin birth which Leni is fully able to comprehend after her experience. The *Verf.* calls this experience by its theological name, *Seinserfüllung*, drawing a typological parallel to the Annunciation. The name Eva comes from the Hebrew word for "life" and alludes to the attraction she holds for all men carrying with it an Eve like carnal element. In the *Vorbemerkung* Böll states that Eva Kreyl-Print and Katharina Richter "könnten Fernsehansagerinnen sein" (p. 15). These women are both, like Leni and Katharina Blum before them, desired by many men and can only be possessed by those men for whom they experience an instinctive feeling, a spontaneous attraction. This "typisch Böllsche Liebesbegegnung" is "zufällig, tiefgreifend und in Katharinas (Blum) Worten-fast religiös überhöht:[12] 'Mein Gott, er war es eben, der da kommen soll, und ich hätte ihn geheiratet und Kinder mit ihm gehabt'" (*Katharina Blum*, p. 61).

The name Elisabeth stems from the Hebrew word meaning "my God is perfection" and alludes to the religious nature of woman and her unwillingness to compromise truth. This leads to the demise of the character (Elisabeth), who ends her life rather than to fall victim to the political powers.

Religion is not found in the institution of the church, but rather exists

---

[11]*Frankfurter Vorlesungen*, p. 100.

[12]Jochen Vogt. *Heinrich Böll*. Munich: C.H. Beck, 1987, p. 128.

exclusively within Böll's women themselves. Böll is very clear in his criticism of the Church through the character of Heinrich Kreyl. Heinrich has attended church services every Sunday for "solange ich mich erinnern kann, bin ich gern in den Gottesdienst gegangen. Man brauchte mich nie zu zwingen, es war zwar Pflicht, aber ich hab's nie als solche empfunden, und während des Krieges und nachher war's ein noch größerer Trost--und ein Bedürfnis. Aber seit gestern . . ." (p. 230). In Böll's earlier works, his characters often sought refuge in convents, or through prayer, but now these places no longer offer solace or consolation. The Church has become an institution that rubber stamps the political powers and merely serves as a place that one attends on Sunday and on special occasions. "Die Kirche hat ausgedient--hierzuland. Chundt und alle anderen, auch schon Erftler, *sie haben sie ausgesaugt, leer gesaugt,* sie brauchen sie jetzt kaum noch" (p. 186). The innocent Katharina reacts vehemently upon the mere mention of the word church : "Es tut mir weh, daß so ein Mädchen wie Katharina *sich schüttelt,* wenn sie von der Kirche nur hört" (p. 216).

Katharina comes from the Greek word for "pure" one and refers to the innocence that woman is able to maintain and exude despite participation in a society with which they are in conflict. In his previous works Böll had undertaken the task to capture the three-fold nature of woman in his heroines. Böll continues this task with marked changes that have significant implications and serve as valuable insights for possible interpretations of his final work and the philosophy he espouses therein.

Frauen vor Flußlandschaft is written in monologue and dialogue form as the subtitle indicates *Roman in Dialogen und Selbstgesprächen.* Upon reading the novel, the reader has the impression that it is a drama.[13] Böll claims to have used this perspective in order to remove himself, the

---

[13]*Frauen vor Flußlandschaft* Präsentiert sich, strenggenommen, als Lesedrama, die Erzählerfunktion ist auf Regieanweisungen reduziert (Vogt, p. 152).

author, from the story.[14]

Topics of the Catholic Church, marriage and politics are the main focus of the dialogues among the characters. Böll depicts present German society as nothing more than an extension of the Nazi period in German history. Power rests in the hands of a political elite, who manipulate the public, media and masses behind the scenes.

The women associated with this political elite are highlighted in this novel. The backdrop of the novel is the Rhine river, no longer the "pure"(rein-Rhein) seat of the new democracy that was to thrive there. The Rhine serves as the last refuge for the women figures, most notably Erika Wubler. She watches the Rhine river from her balcony. It is the only form of consolation she can find in the harsh reality of her life. It serves as the only escape from a society and political system that she can no longer tolerate. Wives who become too knowledgable about political matters are sent to mental institutions and are slowly driven to suicide as seen in the character of Elisabeth Blaukrämer. No one believes her real experiences and she is labeled an exaggerator and "insane." She is isolated in a "luxury" hotel (*Gästehaus Kuhlbollen*), which is occupied by women only, to protect her. In reality she is constrained there to protect the political elite from the truth of her statements that could prove fatal for those in power.

The women vividly recall the horrors of the Nazi past unlike their male counterparts who have "systematische (*ihre*) Erinnerung geschlachtet (*Haus ohne Hüter*)." The women who have experienced the war and the Nazi past "können nicht vergessen." Many of the wives become victims of their men's ambitious career goals and are "abgeschoben in Villen, Sanatorien, eine ging aus eigenem Entschluß in

---

[14]The novel consists of glimpses of life of politically powerful men seen through the eyes of their wives, girlfriends and companions. The dialogues and monologues take place in bedrooms, at parties and on terraces of their residences that overlook the Rhine.

den Rhein"[15] because they are a threat to exposing their ties and involvement to the Nazi regime. The older women characters are a constant reminder to their powerful husbands of their guilt and real natures.

The Rhine serves as the muse for the lengthy monologues of Erika Wubler and Eva Kreyn-Plint. Heinrich Kreyn's wife had ended her life by walking into the Rhine "Ich habe mir immer vorgestellt, sie hätte bleierne Schuhe an den Füßen und wanderte, wanderte weiter, rheinabwärts, auf die Nordsee zu . . . Der Rhein lockte sie mehr als Erftler-Blums Nachkriegsdeutschland" (p. 100). Eva goes on to contemplate such an end herself "'In den Rhein gehen' -- ein schöner Ausdruck -- eines Tages tu ich's vielleicht auch" (p. 100). The only alternative to survival seems to be to lead the life of an outsider as depicted in the characters of Katharina Richter and Karl von Kreyn. They choose an alternative lifestyle, live in a trailer home without benefit of marriage. Katharina, "ein kluges, analystisch begabtes Kind," (p. 53), is the survivor among the group of women, by whom she is surrounded. She can, however not change the situation as it exists because she does not have, nor desires to have the political power to make changes. The younger females, such as Katharina Richter, are either "Aussteiger" who have rejected their politically powerful families or noble backgrounds, or working class women who possess moral integrity and who are unwilling to compromise this integrity for power and money.

Böll's frustration with the present German society finds its best echo in the character of Professor Tucherer. He is a very learned man who has benefitted from intense study of the history and philosophy of man and wishes to share his insights and knowledge with the political forces that are in power. He is, however, only listened to by the wives of the powerful politicians whose interests lie in "Altbaumarkt und ihren Kindern . . .

---

[15]Vogt, p. 152.

Porzellan, Papageien und Antiquitäten" (p. 201-202). Professor Tucherer becomes extremely "niedergeschlagen, daß sich keiner hier für das interessiert, was er mitzuteilen wünscht, sondern nur für seinen Namen" (p. 200). Katharina observes the sad Professor and thinks: "wie kommt er aber auch dazu, Grete Chundt Sartre ausreden zu wollen, den ihr nie jemand einzureden versucht hat. Sie weiß von Sartre nur, daß er schmutzige Fingernägel hatte" (p. 201). The frustration that Professor Tucherer is experiencing, parallels Katharina's resignation regarding the society she lives in. The men in power are not moved by the wisdom of the ages, but by personal agendas of money (Chundt and Schwamm) and power. Tucherer, like the women in the company of such men, is nothing more than a decorative "Anhängsel" to give intellectual and human credence to the political arena. The way women rebel against such an existence is to choose not to have children, by committing genealogical suicide, or by not having legitimate children. Like the Catharists, who condemned marriage since it led to children and thus entrapped more spiritual souls in evil, material bodies (see page 118), Böll's women refuse to contribute to a continuation of the evil in the society in which they live.

Katharina refuses to marry Karl, the father of her child, because the child would then inherit a title of nobility. This would lend an air of legitimacy to a society of which she cannot approve. Katharina, like Katharina Blum before her, is striving to better her education and position in society, but not by compromising her private virtue. She is working on a doctoral dissertation "über die Rolle des Geldes im Werk von Balzac und Dostojewski. Bei dem Thema finde ich Übergänge zum Bankfact und kann sogar die Dritte Welt noch reinwürgen" (p. 201). As Leni and Katharina Blum before her, she will follow her internal moral compass even if this threatens her very existence. She is not guided by external ceremonies, or institutions such as marriage and the Church, but rather acts in accordance with her own moral dictates. As in *Fürsorgliche Belagerung* and *Katharina*

Blum, her lover Karl von Kreyl and she are unable to find a new life in the present society. A strong tone of resignation is evident in Böll's last three novels (*Katharina Blum, Fürsorgliche Belagerung, Frauen vor Flußlandschaft*). The truly decent few become outsiders (*Aussteiger*) and live separated from the rest of society surrounded by a small "group" of supporters.

Böll's narrative perspective underscores an ever-increasing sense of resignation that he feels with contemporary society. There is an evolutionary nature to the development of this narrative point of view that parallels Bölls increasing disenchantment with contemporary society. Already in *Billard um halbzehn* Böll attempted to make narrated history seem alive by incorporating a montage of various monologues and remembrances without the interference of a narrator. In *Gruppenbild mit Dame* the role of the narrator was relegated to a gatherer of facts. Böll made use of recollections, interviews, protocols, reports as well as subjective judgments and assumptions on the part of the "witnesses" who recalled details of Leni's life. By providing a multi-leveled complex and often contradictory portrait of Leni, Böll underscores the complexity of the character and "so wird das Geflecht des fiktive Biographischen intensiver und, wenn man so will, glaubwürdiger."[16] Vogt concludes "man kann also vorläufig vermuten, daß die Art der Figurenzeichnung, die Erzählweise überhaupt mit den inhaltlichen Bestimmungen, dem Charakter der Zentralfigur zusammenhängt: weil diese der glatten und bruchlosen Einpassung ins gesellschaftliche System sich sperrt, ist sie nicht eindeutig und bruchlos zu charakterisieren."[17]

The dialogue and monologue form of Böll's last and final novel allows the reader to be thrown into the direct thoughts of the characters.

---

[16]Karl Heinz Bohrer. *Frankfurter Allgemeine Zeitung*. February 2, 1972, p. 154.

[17]Vogt, pp. 107-108.

Like Professor Tucherer talking to the wives of the politicians, the conversations become banal and meaningless "Angesichts der Resignation wird jede Fabel, jedes Erzählen belanglos, letztlich unnötig, deshalb erzählte Böll auch nicht mehr, sondern griff zur Dialogform."[18]

Women still serve as sounding boards for their men in times of turmoil and provide their men with a nurturing and caring environment, but conflict arises when the "Treue" for the spouse conflicts with that of the political boss (p. 93). Their voices find very little resonance, or echo in a world "ausgesaugt, leer gesaugt" (p. 186) of humanity, virtue and values. The positive women provide a personal refuge for their men who have compromised their principles to rise in the system. The women do not, however, compromise their private virtue and thereby retain a sense of "innocence" in their being.[19] Men are drawn to these women (Erika, Eva, Katharina), but they cannot be like them.[20]

Evolution of Woman

Böll's ideal woman as depicted in his works has undergone an evolutionary process. Whereas the male heroes have remained relatively static, the women have undergone a significant change. The woman has moved from the periphery of the early works to the central role, marked by important changes in her make-up. This shift in the latest works marks a significant literary break. When the male dominated the action, the anger and hostility toward the status quo was Böll's major concern. With the appearance of *Gruppenbild mit Dame* and *Die verlorene Ehre der Katharina Blum*, Böll suggests an alternative solution to withdrawal and isolation. He encourages an active participation of the *Lämmer* in the

---

[18]Falkenstein, p. 80.

[19]"Das Ineinander von Frömmigkeit und Weltverantwortung hat der Schriftsteller (Böll) am deutlichsten in Frauengestalten dargestellt." (Neilen, p. 123).

[20]"Böll's Frauenlob steht gegen 'die Lächerlichkeit des Mannes.'" (*Erinnerung*, p. 542).

society of *Büffel* (Katharina, Abfallfahrer). In Böll's final works *Fürsorgliche Belagerung* and *Frauen vor Flußlandschaft*, Böll focuses on women figures of virtue, who shine in an evil world and illuminate the vice around them. Woman attests to the fact that private virtue can endure the worst afflictions and survive with innocence intact.

She has taken on some characteristics during her evolution. She has become assertive and efficient, but in combination with her loving and compassionate nature, she has achieved a harmony of self. Love still rules her actions and nature, and thus she has maintained her traditional womanly traits. But she has emerged strong in her refusal to compromise her individual virtue and to participate in a profit-oriented, greedy society. She is restored by Böll as a model of virtue, one for men to follow. She is able to survive all that confronts her, and this ability to survive represents for Böll the only sanctioned self-assertion.

Böll, in the tradition of the European humanists of Dante and Goethe, sings the praises of womanhood in his song of innocence. Whatever the changes in mythical, religious and artistic interpretations of the eternal feminine, one constant always remains: men imagine her able to endure and overcome whatever confronts her.

Bibliography

I. Primary Works

Heinrich Böll. *Brief an einen jungen Katholiken*. Cologne: Kiepenheuer and Witsch, 1961.

_____. *Das Brot der frühen Jahre*. Frankfurt am Main: Ullstein Verlag, 1963.

_____. *Hierzulande: Aufsätze zur Zeit*. Munich: Deutscher Taschenbuch Verlag, 1963.

_____. *Ansichten eines Clowns*. Munich: Deutscher Taschenbuch Verlag, 1963.

_____. *Zum Tee bei Dr. Borsig*. Munich: Deutscher Taschenbuch Verlag, 1964.

_____. *Der Zug war pünktlich*. Frankfurt am Main. Ullstein Verlag, 1965.

_____. *Frankfurter Vorlesungen*. Cologne: Kiepenheuer and Witsch, 1966.

_____. *Nicht nur zur Weihnachtszeit*. Munich: Deutscher Taschenbuch Verlag, 1966.

_____. *Aufsätze, Kritiken, Reden*. Cologne: Kiepenheuer and Witsch, 1967.

_____. *Wanderer, kommst du nach Spa . . .* Munich: Deutscher Taschenbuch Verlag, 1967.

_____. *Hausfriedensbruch*. Cologne: Kiepenheuer and Witsch,

_____. *Haus ohne Hüter*. Frankfurt am Main: Ullstein Verlag 1969.

_____. *Wo warst du, Adam?* Frankfurt am Main: Ullstein, 1970.

_____. *Gruppenbild mit Dame*. Cologne: Kiepenheuer and Witsch, 1971.

_____. *Und sagte kein einziges Wort*. Frankfurt am Main: Ullstein, 1972.

_____. *Erzählungen 1950-1970*. Cologne: Kiepenheuer and Witsch, 1973.

_____. *Neue politische und literarische Schriften*. Cologne: Kiepenheuer and Witsch, 1973.

_____. *Billard um halbzehn, Ansichten eines Clowns, Ende einer Dienstfahrt*. Cologne: Kiepenheuer and Witsch, 1974.

_____. "Deutsche Meisterschaft." *Text und Kritik* 33 (1974).

_____. *Die verlorene Ehre der Katharina Blum*. Cologne: Kiepenheuer and Witsch, 1974.

_____. *Drei Tage in März*. Cologne: Kiepenheuer and Witsch, 1975.

_____. *Berichte zur Gesinnungslage der Nation*. Hamburg: Rowohlt, 1977.

_____. *Einmischung Erwünscht: Schriften zur Zeit*. Cologne: Kiepenheuer and Witsch, 1977.

_____. *Fälle für den Staatsanwalt*. Salzburg: Residenz, 1978.

_____. *Fürsorgliche Belagerung*. Cologne: Kiepenheuer and Witsch, 1979.

_____. *Was soll aus dem Jungen bloss werden?* Bornheim-Merten: Lamuv Verlag, 1981.

_____. *Das Vermächtnis*. Bornheim-Merten: Lamuv Verlag, 1982.

_____. *Vermintes Gelände: Essayistische Schriften 1977-1981.* Cologne: Kiepenheuer and Witsch, 1982.

_____. *Bild Bonn Boenisch.* Bornheim-Merten: Lamuv Verlag, 1984.

_____. *Frauen vor Flusslandschaft.* Cologne: Kiepenheuer and Witsch, 1985.

_____. *Die Fähigkeit zu trauern. Schriften und Reden 1983-1985.* Bornheim-Merten: Lamuv, 1986.

II. Secondary Sources

Angebert, Jean Michel. *The Occult and the Third Reich.* Trans. Lewis A.M. X Sumberg. New York: McGraw Hill, 1975.

Arnold, Heinz Ludwig. "Heinrich Böll's Roman *Gruppenbild mit Dame.*" *Text und Kritik.* Volume 33. Munich: Richard Boorberg, 1971.

_____. "Im Gespräch mit Heinz Ludwig Arnold." *Text und Kritik.* Munich: Richard Boorberg, 1971.

"Au is a Camera." *Newsweek*, May 14, 1973.

Balzer, Bernd. "Einigkeit der Einzelgänger." In *Die subversive Madonna.* Ed. Renate Matthaei. Cologne: Kiepenheuer and Witsch, 1975, pp. 11-23.

_____. "Humanität als aästhetisches Prinzip -- Die Romane Heinrich Böll's." In *Heinrich Böll. Eine Einführung in das Gesamtwerk in Einzelinterpretationen.* Ed. Hanno Beth. Regensburg: Scriptor Verlag, 1975, pp 1-27.

Beckel, Albrecht. *Mensch, Gesellschaft, Kirche bei Heinrich Böll.* Osnabrück: Fromm, 1966.

Bering-Jensen, Helle. "Böll's Last Novel Is a Fitting Finale." *Insight.* June 27, 1988, pp. 62-63.

Bernath, Arpad. "Zur Stellung des Romans Gruppenbild mit Dame." In *Die subversive Madonna*. Ed. Renate Matthaei. Cologne: Keipenheuer and Witsch, 1975.

Bernhard, Hans Joachim. "Der Clown als Verf." *Neue Deutsche Literatur*, 20 (1972).

_____. *Die Romane Heinrich Böll's*. Berlin: Rutten und Loening, 1970.

_____. "Es gibt sie nicht, und es gibt sie." In *Die subversive Madonna*. Ed. Renate Matthaei. Cologne: Kiepenheuer and Witsch, 1975.

Beth, Hanno. *Heinrich Böll. Eine Einführung in das Gesamtwerk in Einzelinterpretationen*. Kronberg: Scriptor Verlag, 1975.

_____. "Rufmord und Mord: die publizistische Dimension der Gewalt." In *Heinrich Böll*. Ed. Hanno Beth. Kronberg: Scriptor Verlag, 1975.

_____. "Trauer zu dritt und mehreren." *Text und Kritik*. Munich: Richard Boorberg, 1974.

Bienek, Horst. "Heinrich Böll." In *Werkstattgespräche mit Schriftstellern*. Munich: Hanser, 1962, pp. 138-51.

Böll, Heinrich and Dieter Wellershoff. "*Gruppenbild mit Dame*. Ein Tonbandinterview." *Akzente*, 18 (1971).

Borst, Arno. *Die Katharer*. Stuttgart: Hiersemann, 1953.

"Briefly Noted." *The New Yorker*, October 7, 1967, p. 161.

Bronsen, David. "Böll's women: Patterns in male-female relationships " *Monatshefte* 57 (1965), pp 291-300.

Burbach, Ute, Gerhard Kothy, Egbert Schmidt, and Regine Schulz. "Heinrich Böll -- Eine biographische Skizze." In *Heinrich Böll*. Ed. Hanno Beth. Kronberg: Scriptor Verlag, 1975, pp. 151-187.

Burns, Robert A. *The Theme of Non-Conformism in the Works of Heinrich Böll*. University of Warwick Occassional Papers in German Studies, No. 3, 1973.

Carey, Madalynn J. "Virginal Aspects of Female Characters in the Works of Heinrich Böll." Unpublished Master's Report. University of Texas at Austin, 1975.

Carlson, Ingeborg L. "Heinrich Böll's *Gruppenbild mit Dame* als frohe Botschaft der Weltverbindung." *University of Dayton Review*, 11, ii (1973), pp. 51-64.

Chalons, Robert. "L'art du romancier chez Heinrich Böll; notes de lecture." *Allemagne d'aujord'hui*, VII (1957), 681-687.

The Christian Science Monitor, October 20, 1966, p. 10.

Cirlot, J. E. *A Dictionary of Symbols*. New York: Philosophical Library, Inc., 1962. ✗

Collier's Encyclopedia. New York: P. F. Collier, Inc., 1977.

Conrad, Robert C. "An Interpretation of Catholic Thought in the Works of Heinrich Böll." *D.A.I.*, 30: 3084A-85A. (Cincinnati).

_____. "The Humanity of Heinrich Böll's Love and Religion." *Boston University Journal* 21, ii, pp. 35-42.

Coupe, W. A. "Heinrich Böll's 'Und sagte kein einziges Wort'--An Analysis." *German Life and Letters*, 17 (1963-64), pp. 238-49.

Cunliffe, W. J. "Heinrich Böll's Eccentric Rebels." *Humanities Association Bulletin* 25, pp. 2198-303.

Deschner, Margareta. "Böll's 'Lady'": A New Eve." *University of Dayton Review* 11, ii (1973), pp. 11-23.

Durzak, Manfred. "Entfaltung oder Reduktion des Erzählers?" In *Böll. Untersuchungen zum Werk.* Ed. Manfred Jurgensen. Munich: Francke Verlag, 1975.

_____. "Epische Summe? Zur Analyse und Wirkung seines Romans *Gruppenbild mit Dame.* In *Basis. Jahrbuch für deutsche Gegenwartsliteratur.* Ed. Reinhold Grimm and Jost Hermand. Frankfurt am Main: Athenäum Verlag, 1972, pp. 174-197.

_____. "Leistungsverweigerung als Utopie?" In *Die subversive Madonna.* Ed. Genate Matthaei. Cologne: Kiepenheuer and Witsch, 1975, pp. 82-99.

Emery, Richard Wilder. *Heresy and Inquistition in Narbonne.* New York: Columbia U. Press, 1941.

Encyclopedia International. New York: Grolier, 1964.

Enderstein, Carl O. "Heinrich Böll und seine Künstlergestalten." *German Quarterly,* 43 (1970), pp. 733-48.

Enright, D. J. "Cracking Leni's Case." *New York Review of Books,* May 31, 1973.

Falkenstein, Henning. *Heinrich Böll.* Berlin: Colloguium Verlag, 1987.

Ferrante, Joan. *Woman As Image in Medieval Literature.* New York: Columbia U. Press, 1975.

Fleming, Alice. "Heinrich Böll." *Intellectual Digest,* May 3, 1975, pp. 64-65.

Friedrichsmeyer, Erhard. "Böll's Satires." *University of Dayton Review,* 10 (1974-75), pp. 5-10.

157

Gardner, Edmund G. *St. Catherine of Siena*. London: J.M. Dent and Co., 1907.

Gies, Frances and Joseph. *Women in the Middle Ages*. New York: Thomas Y. Crowell Co., 1978.

Giordani, Igino. *Saint Catherine of Siena*. Trans. Thomas J. Tobin. Boston: Paulist Press, 1959.

Grothe, Wolfgang. "Biblische Bezüge im Werk Heinrich Bölls." *Studia Neophilologica*, 45 (1973), pp. 306-322.

Grothmann, Wolhelm H. "Die Rolle der Religion im Menschenbild Heinrich Bölls." *The German Quarterly*, 44 (1971), pp. 191-207.

Grützbach, Fred, ed. *Heinrich Böll. Freies Geleit für Ulrike Meinhof: ein Artikel und seine Folgen*. Cologne: Kiepenheuer and Witsch, 1972.

Guirdham. *The Great Heresy*. Jersey: Neville Spearman, 1977.

Hartlaub, Geno. "Metaphysisch, Religiös." *Frankfurter Hefte*, 10 (1971), pp. 793-194.

_____. "Recherchen nach dem guten Menschen." *Frankfurter Hefte*, 26 (1971), pp. 789-794.

Hartung, Rudolf. "Heinrich Böll/*Gruppenbild mit Dame*." *Neue Rundschau*, 82 (1971), p. 757.

Hättich, Edgar. "Heinrich Böll." In *Schriftsteller der Gegenwart. Deutsche Literatur. 53 Porträts*. Ed. Klaus Nonenmann. Olten: Walter, 1963, pp. 58-64.

Heer, Friedrich. *The Intellectual History of Europe*. London: Weidenfals and Nicolson, Ltd., 1966.

Heer, Friedrich. *The Medieval World*. Trans. Janet Sonderheimer. New York: Mentor Books, 1962.

Heiney, Donald. *The Christian Science Monitor*, September 30, 1965, p. 11.

Heissenbüttel, Helmut and Hans Schwab-Felisch. "Wie man dokumentarisch erzählen kann. Zwei Stimmen zu Heinrich Böll's neuem Roman." *Merkur* 25 (1971), pp. 911-916.

Hengst, Heinz. "Die Frage nach der 'Diagonale zwischen Gesetz und Barmherzigkeit."' In *Text und Kritik* 33 (1974), pp. 17-26.

Hirsch, Suzanne. *Heinrich Böll's Female Trinity and the Restauration: Evolution of a Response.* Diss. University of Texas at Austin 1976.

Hoffmann, Leopold. *Heinrich Böll. Einführung in Leben und Werk.* Luxembourg: St. Paulus, 1965.

Holmes, Edmond. *The Albigensian or Catharist Heresy.* London: Williams and Norgate, Ltd., 1925.

Huffzky, Karin. "Die Hüter und ihr Schrecken vor der Sache. Das Mann-Frau-Bild in den Romanen von Heinrich Böll." Ed. Hanno Beth. *Heinrich Böll. Eine Einführung in das Gesamtwerk in Einzelinterpretationen.* Regensburg: Scriptor Verlag, 1975, pp. 2g-54.

Interpretationen zu Heinrich Böll. Kurzgeschichten I. Munich: Oldenbourg Verlag, 1970.

"Interview von Reich-Ranicki (1967)." In *Heinrich Böll: Aufsätze, Kritiken Reden.* Cologne: Kiepenheuer and Witsch, 1967.

Jurgensen, Manfred, ed. *Böll. Untersuchungen zum Werk.* Munich: Francke Verlag, 1975.

Just, Georg. "Ästhetik des Humanen -- oder Humanum ohne Ästhetik? Zur Heiligenlegende von der Leni G.." In *Böll. Untersuchungen zum Werk.* Ed. Manfred Jurgensen. Bern: Francke Verlag, 1975, pp. 55-76.

159

Kafitz, Dieter. "Formtradition und religiöses Ethos: Zur Realismuskonzeption Heinrich Böll's." *Der Deutschunterricht*, 28 (1975), pp. 69-85.

Kalow, Gert. "Heinrich Böll." In *Christliche Dichter der Gegenwart*. Ed. Hermann Friedmann and Otto Mann. Heidelberg: Rothe, 1955, pp. 426-35.

Klieneberger, H. R. "Heinrich Böll in *Ansichten eines Clowns*." *German Life and Letters*, 19 (1965-66), pp. 34-9.

Kosler, Hans Christian. "Besinnung auf die Subjekte."*Frankfurter Hefte*, 10 (1971), pp. 791-792.

Kurz, Paul Konrad, S. J. "Recherchen nach dem guten Menschen." *Frankfurter Hefte* 10 (1971), pp. 789-791.

Lange, Victor. "Erzählen als moralisches Geschäft." In *Die subversive Madonna*. Ed. Renate Matthaei. Cologne: Kiepenheuer and Witsch, 1975, pp. 100-122.

Lengning, Werner, ed. *Der Schriftsteller Heinrich Böll: eine biographischbibliographischer Abriss*. Munich: Deutscher Taschenbuchverlag, 1972.

Leonardt, Rudolf Walter. "Das Ende der Resignation." *Die Zeit*, October 31, 1972.

_____. *This Germany. The Story since the Third Reich*. Trans. Catherine Hutter. Middlesex, England: C. Nicholls and Co., Ltd., 1961.

Ley, Ralph. "Compassion, Catholicism and Communism: Reflections on Böll's *Gruppenbild mit Dame*." *University of Dayton Review*, 10, pp. 25-39.

160

Linder, Christian. "Drei Tage im März." Conversations with Christian Linder. March 11-13, 1975. In *Werke*. Volume 10 Interviews. Cologne, 1978, pp. 348-426.

Locke, Richard. *The New York Times Book Review*, May 6, 1973, pp. 1, 20, 22 .

_____. "Portrait of a Woman, a city and modern Germany -- Heinrich Böll's best novel: *Group Portrait with Lady*." In *New York Times Book Review*, May 6, 1973.

MacPherson, Enid. *A Student's Guide to Böll*. London: Heinemann, 1972.

Madaule, Jacques. *The Albigensian Crusade*. Trans. Barbara Wall. New York: Fordham U. Press, 1967.

Maddocks, Melvin. "Heinrich Böll's Song of Innocence." *Altantic Monthly*, July, 1973.

Martin, Werner. *Heinrich Böll. Eine Bibliographie seiner Werke*. New York: Georg Olms Verlag, 1975.

Maslow, Abraham. *Toward a Psychology of Being*. Princeton: Van Nostrand, 1962.

Matthaei, Renate. *Die subversive Madonna. Ein Schlüssel zum Werk Heinrich Böll's*. Cologne: Kiepenheuer and Witsch, 1975.

Maynard, Theodore. "St. Catherine of Siena. The Ecstatic Politician." In *Saints for Our Times*. Garden City, New York: Doubleday and Co., Inc., 1952.

Meyer, Herman. *Der Sonderling in der deutschen Dichtung*. Munich: Hanser Verlag, 1963.

Michaelis, Rolf. "Der gute Mensch von Gemmelsbroich. Heinrich Böll's Erzählung *Die verlorene Ehre der Katharina Blum.*" Die Zeit, August 9, 1974.

Migner, Karl. "Heinrich Böll." In *Deutsche Literatur der Gegenwart in Einzeldarstellungen.* Ed. Dietrich Weber. Stuttgart: Kröner Verlag, 1976.

Molling, Heinrich. *Heinrich Böll -- eine 'christliche' Position?* Zurich: Juris Verlag, 1974.

Moore, R. I. *The Birth of Popular Heresy.* London: Butler and Tanner, Ltd., 1975.

Morewedge, Rosmarie Thee, Ed. *The Role of Woman in the Middle Ages.* Albany: State U. of New York Press, 1975.

Nägele, Rainer. *Heinrich Böll: Einführung in das Werk und in die Forschung.* Frankfurt: Fischer, 1976.

Neis, Edgar. *Erläuterungen zu Heinrich Böll's Romane, Erzählungen, Kurzgeschichten.* Hollfeld: Bange, 1966.

Nielen, Manfred. *Frömmigkeit bei Heinrich Böll.* Annweiler: Thomas Plöger Verlag, 1987.

Nobbe, Annemaried. *Heinrich Böll* (Eine Bibliographie seiner Werke und der Literatur über ihn). Cologne: Greven, 1961.

Oldenbourg, Zoe. *Massacre at Montsegur.* New York: George Weidenfeld and Nicolson, Ltd., 1961.

Petersen, Jürgen. "Gruppenbild mit Dame." *Neue Deutsche Hefte*, 131 (1971), p. 141.

Pickar, Gertrud B. "The Impact of Narrative Perspective on Character Portrayal in three Novels of Heinrich Böll: *Billard um halbzehn, Ansichten eines Clowns,* and *Gruppenbild mit Dame.*" *University of Dayton Review,* 11 (1974). pp. 25-35.

Plant, Richard. *The New York Times Book Review,* October 17, 1955 and November 13, 1955.

_____. "The World of Heinrich Böll." *German Quarterly,* 33 (1960), pp. 125-31.

Plard, Henri. "La guerre et l'apres-guerre dans les recits de Heinrich Böll." *Europe II* (1957), pp. 1-19.

_____. "Mut und Bescheidenheit. Krieg und Nachkrieg im Werk Heinrich Bölls." *Der Schriftsteller Heinrich Böll.* Ed. Werner Lengning. Cologne: Kiepenheuer and Wirsch, 1959. pp. 41-64.

Potoker, E. M. *The Saturday Review,* September 11, 1965, p. 42.

Power, Eileen. *Medieval Women.* Ed. M. M. Postan. Cambridge: Cambridge U. Press, 1975.

"Raking the Muck." Heinrich Böll's *Die verlorene Ehre der Katharina Blum.*" Times Literary Supplement, October 11, 1974.

Reich-Ranicki, Marcel, ed. *In Sachen Böll.* Cologne: Kiepenheuer and Witsch, 1968.

_____. "Nachdenken über Leni G." *Die Zeit,* August 10, 1971.

Reid, James H. "Böll's Names." *Modern Language Review,* 69 (1974), pp. 575-83.

_____. Heinrich Böll. *Withdrawal and Reemergence.* London: Wolff, 1973.

_____. "Time in the Works of Heinrich Böll." *Modern Language Review*, 62 (1967). pp. 476-85.

Rieck, Werner. "Heinrich Böll in der Rolle des Rechercheurs--Gedanken zur Erzählweise in Roman *Gruppenbild mit Dame*." *WZPHP*, 18, (1974), pp. 249-255.

Robinson, Walter L. "Heinrich Böll's Indifferent Heroes." Ed. Walter C. Kraft. *Pacific N. W. Conference on Foreign Languages*, 25 (1974).

Runciman, Steven. *The Medieval Manichee*. New York: Viking Press, 1961.

Schütte, Wolfram. "Muss das grosse Schisma fortgesetzt werden? Interview Wolfram Schüttes mit Heinrich Böll." *Frankfurter Rundschau*, November 23, 1974.

Schwarz, Wilhelm Johannes. *Der Erzähler Heinrich Böll*. Bern: Francke, 1967.

_____. "Heinrich Böll." *Christliche Dichter im 20. Jahrhundert Beiträge zur europäischen Literatur*. Ed. Otto Mann. Bern: Francke, 1968, pp. 432-441.

Sharma, Krishna. "Heinrich Böll: An Appreciation." *Journal of the School of Languages*, 3 (1975), pp. 89-98.

Sokel, Walter Herbert. "Perspective and Dualism in the Novels of Böll." *The Contemporary Novel in German: A Symposium*. Ed. Robert R. Heitner. Austin: U. of Texas Press, 1967, pp. 9-36.

Stewart, Keith. "The American Reviews of Heinrich Böll: A Note on the Problems of the Compassionate Novelist." *University of Dayton Review*, 11 (1974).

Stresau, Hermann. *Heinrich Böll*. Berlin: Literarisches Colloquium, 1964.

Struck, Karin and Heinrich Böll. "Schreiben und Lesen." In *Einmischung Erwünscht*. Cologne: Kiepenheuer and Witsch, 1977.

Tern, Jurgen. "Heinrich Böll und seine Kritiker." *Frankfurter Hefte*, 27 (1972). pp. 158-161.

Tierney, Briam and Sidney Painter. *Western Europe in the Middle Ages 300-1475*. New York: Alfred A. Knopf, 1974.

Turberville, A. S. *Medieval Heresy and the Inquisition*. London: Archon Books, 1964.

Uhlig, Gudrun. *Autor, Werk und Kritik. Heinrich Böll, Günter Grass, Uwe Johnson*. Munich: Max Hueber Verlag. p. 969.

Vogt, Jochen. *Heinrich Böll*. Munich: C. H. Beck, 1978.

_____. *Heinrich Böll*. Munich: C.H. Beck, 1987 (Second Edition).

_____. "Vom armen H. B., der unter die Literaturpädagogen gefallen ist." *Text und Kritik* 33 (1974), pp. 32-40.

Wahlberg, Rachel Conrad. *Jesus According to Woman*. New York: Paulus Press, 1975.

Waidson, H. M. "Heroine and Narrator in Heinrich Böll's *Gruppenbild mit Dame*." *FMLS*, 9 (1973), pp. 123-31.

_____. "Die Romane und Erzählungen Heinrich Böll's." *Der Schriftsteller, Heinrich Böll: eine biopraphisch-bibliographischer Abriss*. Ed. Werner Lengning. Cologne: Kiepenheuer and Witsch, 1959.

Wakefield, Walter L. *Heresy, Crusade and Inquisition in Southern France 1100-1250*. Berkeley: U. of California Press, 1974.

Wintzen René. "Eine deutsche Erinnerung." Interview with René Wintzen. October, 1976, In *Werke*. Volume 10 Interviews. Cologne, 1978, pp. 504-665.

Wirth, Günter. *Das christliche Menschenbild bei Böll und Bobrowski.* Berlin: Union Verlag, 1969.

_____. *Heinrich Böll. Essayistische Studie über religiöse und gesellschaftliche Motive im prosawerk des Dichters.* Cologne: Pahl-Rugenstein, 1969.

Wolff, Geoffrey. "Still Life." *Time*, May 28, 1973.

Yuill, W. E. "Heinrich Böll." *Essays in Contemporary German Literature.* Ed. Brian Keith-Smith. London: Wolff, 1966, pp. 141-58.

Ziolkowski, Theodore. "Albert Camus and Heinrich Böll." *Modern Language Notes*, 77 (1962), pp. 282-91.

_____. "Heinrich Böll: Conscience and Craft." *Books Abroad*, 34 (1960), pp. 213-222.

_____. "Typologie und 'Einfache Form' in *Gruppenbild mit Dame.*" *In Die subversive Madonna.* Ed. Renate Matthaei. Cologne Kiepenheuer and Witsch, 1976, pp. 123-140.

Index

168